The 2022 Guide to Side Hustle

Proven online and offline strategies to make extra money in your spare time

Mark Davies

UP

URANUS
PUBLISHING

Uranus Publishing

Contents

One

INTRODUCTION

M illions of Americans have lost their jobs due to the Covid-19 pandemic, as have many small stores and restaurants. At the same time, it has become a hotbed of creativity and the growth of new businesses. According to U.S. Census reports, the number of new businesses in the United States increased by approximately 42 percent in 2020.

You don't have to leave your day job to start a company, as many Americans have discovered. Now it is an excellent time to start a side hustle — a small business that you can run in addition to your full-time job. Thanks to the changes that have occurred regarding the concept of jobs in the modern society, and the substantial advances in new technology, earning a side income has become much easier than it has been in years.

Creating a side business is one of the most prudent financial decisions you can make right now. With the economy in shambles, no one can afford not to diversify their income sources. Even jobs that have always been considered safe have been subject to layoffs and corporate restructuring.

According to a recent report by MBO Partners, a supplier of back-office services to independent contractors, 56 percent of Americans said they would be more comfortable working for themselves than in a conventional job in 2020, up from 32 percent in 2011. Women, people of color, and older employees have been hit the hardest by employment loss during the pandemic, so relying on a job as your primary source of income is definitely dangerous right now.

If you've ever wanted to make more money, pay off debt faster, or save for a holiday, a side hustle is the right choice for you. "Side hustles" are any types of work done in addition to full-time jobs.

Although full-time workers have been doing second (or even third) jobs for generations, side hustles have become more popular in recent years, owing largely to the gig economy.

The gig economy is all about self-directed freelance work and part-time jobs that allow you to work as much (or as little) as you want. As technology enables customers to communicate more directly with a willing workforce, new possibilities for short-term gigs have become more popular. Furthermore, side jobs have become a legitimate and even appropriate way for employees to supplement their full-time income.

Even if you are not concerned about losing your career, a side hustle can be a great source of extra income to help you pay off debt, save money, and even invest. It can also have tax benefits. If you make purchases for your business, you might be able to subtract them from your taxes. Aside from that, a side hustle may be the perfect way to get a glimpse of a potential business you might want to pursue later.

In this book, I've condensed my twenty years of experience as a consultant and over ten years of knowledge gained as a freelancer. At the end of the reading, you will have all the information you need in order to successfully start your own side hustle without running into the typical mistakes made by newbies.

Are you ready to change your life by achieving the financial independence you've always dreamed of?

Let's get started!

Two

WHY YOU SHOULD START A SIDE HUSTLE

A side hustle is a job that you can do in addition to your regular job. It is a flexible second career that pays well, but it is usually something you are passionate about that you do not get to pursue in your primary job. Perhaps it will help you build skills for your primary profession, but more often than not, it will simply be something you enjoy doing.

You may decide to start a side business for a variety of reasons. Let's take a look at the main ones!

Increase and Diversify Your Income

Right now, I want you to consider your financial objectives. Do you want to repay your student loans? Have you paid off your credit card debt? Do you like to give your children a financially secure future? Do you want to take that trip you've talked so much about with your wife?

Those are great targets, but here's the catch: there's just so much money to go around. With your current earnings, it might take you decades to reach your goals.

You could start earning $500, $1,000, $2,000, or more every month if you choose only one of the thousands of side hustle ideas available. The money will help you pay off debts, make retirement payments, and do other things.

I've also heard many personal finance enthusiasts suggest that when deciding whether to pay off debt or save, you should "do what the numbers tell you to do." Although I am a big proponent of paying off student loans and other high-interest debt as soon as possible, I do agree with the point to some extent.

But what I don't think the numbers approach takes into account is the psychological impact of getting tens of thousands of dollars owed to someone else, hanging over your head like a dark cloud.

Debt stinks. It's more than a number, it's a burden that undermines our self-esteem to the core. Debt does not make us feel at peace with ourselves, and it affects our lives unbearably.

Side hustles will help you get rid of the tension and anxiety induced by the debts much faster. You save money on interest charges, and you will be able to put some money into an emergency fund to avoid potential debt, and so on. And, to return to the numbers, more capital means you can begin saving faster.

Increase your earnings. It's so easy.

Why You Need to Diversify Your Income

It wasn't long ago that achieving income diversification and financial security meant nothing more than working for the same business for decades while saving for retirement. Those who were particularly financially savvy meant retiring after 40 years and possibly taking a part-time job at a nearby supermarket to keep finances secure.

However, in today's economy, shielding your finances leads to a more active method of income diversification. In reality, your money is at risk unless you arrange for several income generators and financial backups.

Creating a side business or freelance service is one of the most secure ways to diversify your earnings. A side business requires some effort, but treating it as an entrepreneurial endeavor will pave the way for you to continue making extra money whenever you need it.

Remember! If you are wise and handle more than one source of income, you have a real chance of living the life you've always dreamed of. The more time and effort you put into diversifying your sources of income, the more likely it is that you will gain financial independence and be able to enjoy the life you want.

You Have More Time Than You Think

One of the most common deterrents to starting a side hustle is a perceived lack of time. I understand. You work all day, cook dinner when you get home, do laundry, pack your lunch for the next day, and so on.

And maybe you don't have enough time — those are legitimate cases. However, I will argue that in most circumstances, this is not the case.

Here's why I believe you have more time than you think: the average person spends almost two hours a day on social media. That includes social media platforms such as Facebook, YouTube, and Instagram. Believe me, I do it as well. What if you wanted to divert one hour of your social media time to a side hustle? That is just one hour a day.

And, yes, there are side hustle ideas that can give you a decent living by working just one hour per day. VIPKid is a great side hustle for this, and here's why:

- You teach English online in 25-minute increments.
- It costs $15-$20 per hour, which includes all lesson preparation.
- You decide how many hours you want to work.

If you work this side hustle for one hour five days a week, you can earn an additional $300 to $400 a month. Consider what you will do in two hours!

Simple Ways to Save Time

There are thousands of minor, irrelevant things that someone can do to save time. But now we'll look at how to save time in everyday life by concentrating on general tasks that everybody can do that can make a significant difference in the amount of time needed for what you want to do. Best of all, each of these time-saving strategies is simple to implement. If you complete all ten, you can save so much time that you will be able to start your new side hustle!

• Keep Things in a Regular Place

If you still leave your keys on the table in the hall when you come in, you'll be able to locate them quickly when you leave – and never waste time searching for them. And what works with your keys can work with almost anything else you use daily. It can be your reading glasses or the can opener. Develop the habit of storing the items you use most in one location and returning them to that particular location when you're finished with them.

• Don't Try to Multitask

It is one of the most significant time wasters for the majority of people. Why is it so? According to some experts, multitasking reduces efficiency by approximately 40% – possibly because jumping from one task to another makes it challenging to avoid distractions and can create mental blocks that slow down the development.

• Re-Learn How to Concentrate

Many of us lose a lot of time simply because we're easily distracted - a phenomenon that multitasking exacerbates. Instead of concentrating on one goal and completing it quickly, we cause ourselves to be distracted several times. What was the end result? The initial task takes much longer than it should or should have. Developing the practice of concentrating exclusively on whatever job you're working on and finishing it before moving on to anything else is a perfect way to save time in everyday life.

- Use a calendar to make a list of everything.

It makes no difference if your calendar is electronic or paper. What matters is that you create and retain a single "appointment central", that is a one-stop-shop for everything you need and want to do. This serves two functions: it guarantees you won't forget something important and acts as a to-do list. As opposed to ferrying pieces of paper back to wherever your paper calendar is stored, using a calendar that can come with you (such as a calendar program on a smartphone) saves a significant amount of time.

- Put an end to your procrastination.

Procrastination isn't always a negative thing. What's poor is what happens to everything you're putting off when you finally do it. Problems exacerbate. Misinterpretation multiplies. Trash accumulates. Dealing with problems when they're smaller not only saves time but also makes life easier for you.

- Consolidate Your Chores and Plan Your Trips

Assume you have seven items on your grocery list and, instead of making one trip to the store and purchasing all of them, you make seven different trips, each time purchasing one item. That's what many of us do with our grocery shopping and chores. Instead, plan ahead of time to save time. Some tasks may be completed or picked up on the way to or from work. Alternatively, a ride to one location may be extended to include other nearby stops.

- Learn to Appreciate Routine

Routine is the most effective way to save time in everyday life. My friend Andy goes to the same coffee shop every mid-morning – so often that whoever is working already has his latté ready for him. That's a huge time saver! A routine does not necessarily speed up customer service, but it does make it easier to locate and complete tasks. It also frees up the brain for other tasks, which is a plus.

- Make a meal plan ahead of time

Menu planning ahead of time expedites meal preparation and simplifies grocery shopping. It also makes things less complicated if you're not getting a family meeting on what to eat that night or, worse, having to run out right before dinner to get a missing ingredient.

- Find Out Your Personal Time-Wasters

Personally, I can easily spend 45 minutes deciding what to wear in the morning – all in the name of staying longer in my cozy, comfortable bed. What do you think? When I do it the night before, it takes me less than five minutes – and that includes laying out the clothes. It's typically simple to devise a plan to avoid doing your favorite personal time-wasters once you've identified them.

- Stop worrying

Some of us could potentially increase our life expectancy by 20 years if we could reclaim the time we spend thinking about what could happen or what we've done. Fretting seems to be ingrained in the personalities of specific individuals. Even if we appear to be an average worrisome person, it is still worthwhile to focus on reducing our worrying habits. Aside from saving time, it is much healthier for our general well-being.

Literally, Everyone Can Start a Side Hustle

One of my favorite aspects about side hustles is that there is something for everybody. There is something for all, regardless of education, area of employment, or interests.

The only skill needed for all side hustles is motivation. You can start making stuff happen after you've determined the justification for side hustling, such as paying off debt or retiring early.

Consider starting your own digital marketing agency, which is my all-time favorite side hustle concept. That sounds like a kind of work that would necessitate a degree or experience in marketing, maybe even advertisement. No, no, it's something you can learn to do from the comfort of your own home and raise $1,000 to $2,000+ a month.

Running digital advertising is a legitimate side hustle. See, digital marketing on Facebook is a rising industry as small business owners understand they can attract new customers by leveraging Facebook's vast audience.

However, and this is where you come in, most small business owners do not have the time to practice and implement an effective ad strategy.

Running Facebook advertising is exactly what I did as a side hustle after quitting my teaching job to run this site full-time. I didn't go to marketing school; I learned it on my own and the hard way. But, after landing my first customer, and then another, and another, I was soon out collecting the teacher's salary I had left behind.

I'm not the only one who has had success. Many people have learned and now have this helpful skill after taking the Facebook Side Hustle Course (the course I developed with my buddy Mike Yanda, a lawyer turned digital marketer who now earns $30k a month running Facebook ads).

Many people are working full-time, or even several jobs, raising children, etc., which is why I don't think anyone has time for a side hustle. Some real people studied digital marketing and are now making extra money per month.

But here's the thing: managing Facebook advertising isn't the only ability you can master. On Pinterest, you will learn how to work as a virtual assistant, freelance writer, or make money. Others, such as flipping furniture, make use of skills you most likely already have.

There is enough for everybody out there. Any examples?

Five side jobs that don't need any special skills

Finding a successful side hustle does not require any advanced skills. There are several side hustles that almost everyone can do if they have a smartphone and transportation.

- Animal Walks

If you love animals, one of the most appealing and readily accessible side hustles is dog walking. Rover and Wag are two online sites that will help you find dog-walking jobs that pay between $12 and $15 per half-hour.

Rover is the more freelancer-friendly of the two platforms, with lower fees and the ability for workers to set their own rates. Rover also allows you to build a profile to provide other animal-related services, such as overnight dog sitting.

- Evaluate

Several companies pay freelancers to inspect a product, house, or accident scene and report back on its condition. These websites pay between $5 and $30 per gig, depending on the amount of time and travel involved.

IVueit connects freelancers with commercial property owners who want an on-the-spot analysis of maintenance or repairs. Jobs usually include taking a few pictures and filling out a short form.

Product Tube pays freelancers to record a video of themselves giving a brief product review, either at home or in a shop. This may include comparing two types of snack food or demonstrating how you determine which beer to buy at the grocery store. The videos are usually 2 to 4 minutes long.

- Shop

If you can manage a grocery store, you can shop and deliver groceries for Instacart, Shipt, and Dumpling. Instacart and Shipt hire freelancers to do on-demand shopping for a price that is often dependent on order size. On the other hand, Dumpling assists personal shoppers in managing their own businesses by allowing them to set their own prices and availability.

- Drive

Driving for Lyft and Uber was once a famous side hustle. However, these organizations are continually tinkering with their driver terminology, and the latest regulations are rarely driver-friendly. Fortunately, they are not the only choices.

Alternatives for those who want to make money driving passengers include Zum, Wingz (specialized in pre-scheduled trips from/to airports), HopSkipDrive, and Kango, which book rides for kids who need a lift to/from school, sports, and other youth events. These platforms offer higher hourly rates than any of the ride-hailing behemoths.

Zum, Kango, and HopSkipDrive do require you to have prior experience working with children.

- Baby Sitting

With summer approaching and many parents returning to work, there is a high demand for babysitting services. Long gone is the time when high school students babysat children for a few dollars an hour. Nannies and babysitters should now expect to earn at least minimum wage and, in some cases, up to $25 per hour.

UrbanSitter, Care.com, Bambino, and Sittercity are several websites where you can find a babysitting job.

Ways of Earning Money is Always Changing

If you haven't already guessed, the gig economy is how the future will be. And if you need evidence, consider the following statistics from Upwork's

2019 Freelancing in America Study:

There are currently 58 million freelancers in the United States, an increase of 4 million in the last five years.

- 40% of millennials work as freelancers.
- Freelancing generates about $1 trillion in GDP.
- Freelancing, according to 46% of side hustlers, provides them with more versatility.
- 77% believe technology has made it easier to find jobs.
- 91 percent are optimistic about the future of their business.

In addition, according to a Forbes report, 56 percent of businesses are outsourcing freelance work to side hustlers in order to save money.

By observing these trends, I became convinced of the need to help people in the search for profitable side hustles. Nowadays, we read, play, and work on the internet. The sooner you get started, the easier it will be to learn new technologies and platforms that many online side hustlers use daily.

How the Nature of Work Changes in the Digital Era

We live in a digital world, where rapid technological change is the norm, and it is easier than ever to learn how to make money online.

The world is transitioning to an individual-on-demand economy, which offers fantastic opportunities for entrepreneurship, wealth growth, work-from-home online employment, and time independence.

You could use the Flexjobs app to find a remote job quickly and land some freelance work. Next, use Airbnb to host your own place or to spend months in another world. And you'll be able to do so while saving money relative to your current rent.

Think about it! There are new possibilities everywhere.

Your Side Hustle Can Become Your Main Job

I had no idea when I began this site that blogging would become my full-time work. This is something I've heard from countless freelancers I've worked with over the years.

Most people who have turned their side business into full-time self-employment are enjoying some benefits, including:

- Increased freedom to work where and when you like.

- Rather than being confined to what your typical work pays, you can scale your side hustle to earn more.

- You become your own boss, which I personally enjoy.

At the same time, there are certain downsides of working for yourself, such as the fact that your income can not be as consistent at the beginning. However, this is one of the most compelling reasons to start a side hustle right now. You will increase demand and your client list while maintaining a healthy income from your day job.

The argument is that the choice exists. And it's not called a side hustle for nothing — making a full-time salary from your side hustle takes effort. If quitting your day job is your dream, side hustles are one way to make it a reality.

When to Quit Your Day Job and Go All In With Your Side Hustle

It is not easy to leave your career. It's difficult to substitute the money. You earned your current job and salary after several years of college/training. You had to work your way up the career ladder. You had to work hard and put in the effort. It's not so easy to call it quits. This means you shouldn't expect to go full-time on your side hustle after only one successful weekend. You do not expect a new business concept to generate a full-time income right away. When it comes to starting a successful company, far too many people sell the dream on social media. You get what I mean ... "Earn a living from the beach," or "Look at how this young couple lives in a van and earns one million dollars per month!"

You get the idea. It's frustrating and annoying. It makes you want to give up before you even begin because you can never live up to the hype. For the time being, I want you to forget about all of the success stories. I want you to worry only about yourself. This is your story. You won't be able to build the next Facebook. You can, however, leave your job to start your own company.

What do you need for a side hustle to become your primary source of income?

If you want to leave your job, you'll need *money*. Your company must generate revenue. It would be best if you had investments in the bank and an income from your side hustle, as well as a plan to make even more money to supplement your current income.

Here is a list of reasons why you should not leave your job:

- Self-claimed life coaches
- Motivational quotes
- Expensive courses and workshops
- Another dozen entrepreneurship books to read.

Here's a checklist of what you'll need to quit your job:

Your side hustle has to bring in money.

- Enough money in your bank account to cover unexpected expenditures.
- A strategy for bringing in more money so that you can replace your salary.
- A reduction in spending to help you get through tough times.

How much money do you need to leave your job?

You must save enough money to cover your expenses for at least six months. When you live for yourself, anything is possible. You can experience some financial difficulties. You will need to save money to get through this. You need money to deal with the problems that may arise as an entrepreneur (losing a client overnight or Google wiping out your traffic with one update). There will be days when you don't bring in any money for months. Then there will be times when you feel wealthy because money is pouring in from all sides.

There is no other way out of this. You can't just leave your job because you despise your boss or want to claim the title "CEO" on your social media profiles. You must gain your independence.

You must wait until your side hustle earns more money before you can be fully self-sufficient. Quitting your job would not be easy for the first few weeks. It will cost you many sacrifices, but the reward will be the financial freedom that everyone talks about but few achieve.

If you don't do it, someone else will

There is plenty of room for new side hustlers in the online space, but why let anyone else get a head start earning money that you could be making instead?

People who have already started side hustles have already completed the most difficult part of the process: they took a risk, found a side hustle, and got to work. These individuals have begun to pay off their debts, save for retirement, and diversify their wealth.

To be honest, the toughest part is getting started. There are numerous side hustle opportunities available; all you need to do is find one that interests you and suits your situation. There are side jobs available for teachers, stay-at-home mothers, and others. You have no excuse not to try.

Side hustling is becoming increasingly popular as a viable means of achieving financial objectives. It is as simple as reading a chapter of this book to begin a side hustle today. You should learn about the various options available, choose one that interests you, and get to work.

Don't be that person who wishes they had started a side business last year.

Start earning more money right now!

Three

BEFORE GETTING STARTED

B efore you begin your business, you must first decide if you are permitted to do so under the terms of your employment agreement. Many employers have no rules against running a side business if they do so on their own time and with their equipment.

To be safe, go through the thick stack of paperwork you signed when the company hired you. Some companies may prohibit you from working on side projects for their clients or competitors. If you've misplaced the documents, check to see if your organization has an official website where these agreements are listed or request a copy "for your records" from HR.

When and Where You Will Make Your Side Hustle.

You can make a lot of progress on a side hustle in just a few weeks, but you must schedule time for it so that you can make real progress. Schedule at least one hour a week — or more if you're in a rush to get started — that you're not accountable about something else because it actually happens. Mark a particular activity on your calendar, such as "register web domain" or "research accounting software."

Making a master list of tasks to complete before you begin will help you make the most of your time. Plus, when you cross each one off your list and get closer to your launch, you'll feel a tremendous sense of accomplishment.

Elements to Consider When Choosing a Side Hustle

Starting a side hustle is now easier than ever, but it's worth considering these three factors before diving in headfirst.

Time

You must ensure that any side hustle you choose is appropriate for your time commitments. Some side hustles take a lot more time than others. Blogging, for example, requires a significant amount of time. While it is one of the most lucrative side hustles, it might not be ideal for your lifestyle.

But that doesn't mean you can't find a hustle that meets your requirements. There are several ways to earn extra money; you just need to explore your choices and choose what you are willing to commit to. Here are a few examples of side hustles that don't take up a lot of your valuable time:

- Online Surveys
- Rent out Car/House
- User testing
- eBay Flipping
- Complete tasks on TaskRabbit

Skills

Obviously, the more expertise a side hustle necessitates, the more lucrative it is likely to be. This isn't to say you can't build and learn the skills required for any side hustle you want. It simply means that it may take a little longer before you can jump in and start making money.

Therefore, this is something you should consider carefully. Investing in education is the most effective way to dramatically boost your earnings. And it is here where many people fall short. It's all too tempting to believe that $500 or $1000 is a huge investment that isn't worthwhile.

However, you will be able to build and learn the skills needed to perform a side hustle that will enable you to recoup your initial investment and more. And this is the secret to investing in yourself and your potential opportunity to gain more money.

Passion

Do you have to be enthusiastic about your side hustle choice?

The reality is that it does. And it is incredibly beneficial.

There are many things you might do to supplement your primary source of income. However, chances are you have interests and hobbies. And this might potentially give you an advantage over your competitors.

Consider a music instructor. They work 40 hours a week at a school for regular teacher pay. This is fantastic, but the teacher wishes to better their situation and earn more money. They might now think about starting a blog or running Facebook advertising. Both are excellent side hustles that would be ideal for the job. But, if the music instructor considers their abilities, a perfect side hustle is right in front of them. Giving music lessons on the side allows them to charge a reasonable fee since they are already eligible and can begin immediately.

This may not be the case for everybody, so don't be concerned if you don't have any evident abilities that you can monetize. Remember that talents can be transferred and that there are many side hustle opportunities.

However, getting a passion is a perfect way to get started with side hustling the right way – and it also means you can make more money.

After all, that is what it all boils down to.

How Much Will a Side Hustle Cost You?

Each side hustle has a unique start-up expense. Speaking with people who run similar businesses is the best way to get a sense of what they are. Reach out to them in LinkedIn groups, listen to podcasts about starting a company in a specific niche (you can find them on ListenNotes), or attend free online industry events where you can network and ask questions.

If your side hustle includes freelancing in your current profession, your expenses would most likely be minimal. To get started, you'll need;

- a computer and phone different from the ones you use for work;

- any industry-specific software required;

- and accounting software such as FreshBooks, QuickBooks, or Xero to keep track of your income and expenditures, so you have the records you need to file your taxes correctly.

If you want to represent large corporations, you will also need to create a basic website to pass their compliance tests. They would need proof that you are self-employed and selling yourself so that they do not violate worker classification laws. Many sites, such as WordPress, Wix, and Weebly, allow you to create a simple website for free. You also need to register a URL with GoDaddy or one of its rivals to set up a website.

If you're starting a product-based company, you'll also need a website and possibly some online advertising on Google, Facebook, or other sites. If you do not use a drop-ship model, you must also include inventory and shipping costs. It is necessary to speak with people who run companies in that niche to decide if they fit your needs.

Essential Tools to Set Up Your Side Hustle

Setting up a side hustle business can be difficult, particularly if you already have a full-time job. When you expand a fledgling company on your own, your evenings and weekends become increasingly occupied. Finding the time and energy to do something can seem to be nearly impossible at first.

Doing a side hustle has never been simpler, thanks to the constant advances in software and technology. Even with family obligations, job emergencies, potential health problems, general chores, and the need for enough exercise and sleep, it is possible to develop a thriving side hustle company by leveraging the advantages of modern resources and software.

There are tens of thousands – if not millions – of applications and websites available to entrepreneurs and solopreneurs. Most are designed to make the business owner's life easier in terms of efficiency, workflow, cash flow, communication, and a variety of other areas. And it is some of these techniques that can help transform a good side hustle into a possibility rather than a pipe dream.

If you're just getting started with your own side hustle, the following seven types of resources will make it a lot easier to develop and manage.

Cloud Invoicing

Invoicing is a required task if your side hustle includes dealing with customers. However, with high-quality free invoicing software, such as cloud-based invoicing platform here at Invoice Ninja, you can quickly build and submit invoices.

It is no longer necessary to build an invoice in Excel or Word. Simply change a professionally crafted invoice template, which can then be used repeatedly with your brand colors and logo. All data is automatically monitored, and there are over 40 different payment gateways to choose from, making invoicing a breeze.

Time-tracking

A side hustle needs a significant amount of time to be properly managed, even if it is not your primary job. Every spare minute and hour must be spent wisely and productively. When you have a full-time job and are trying to build a side company, every second matters.

That is why you need effective time-tracking software. When you monitor and evaluate, every minute spent working on your side project – as well as your entire day – you'll easily identify areas where you can increase productivity while minimizing distractions. Time-tracking software is often needed when recording time spent on hourly-priced client projects.

Project management

Project management software, including time-tracking tools, is extremely useful in terms of optimizing workflow, productivity, and peace of mind. And if you work as a solo professional with no team to lead, you will have several tasks to complete each day. Kanban Boards, for example, are project management tools that allow you to quickly see where you are in terms of current progress.

The Kanban Board's visual nature aids your brain in quickly determining what needs to be done and when, as well as what can be assigned, outsourced, deferred, or merged into something else. A good project management system will make things a little easier after a long day at your full-time job.

Cloud storage

One of the worst things you can do as an online business owner is put too much trust in your computer's durability and wellbeing. Storing all of your files on your laptop will function for months, even years before it doesn't. And you've squandered everything in one heinous swoop.

Cloud storage ensures that your important data, such as client work, self-created goods, marketing content, and any course materials you buy, are secure and available regardless of computer failures.

Dropbox, OneDrive, and Google Drive are examples of common cloud storage and file management systems.

CRM - Customer Relationship Management software.

Managing more than a few clients or customers, whether you're selling goods or services, can be difficult. You can only go so far with pen and paper or Excel. That is why, if you want to develop your side hustle quickly and potentially extend it, you need CRM software.

Customer Relationship Management (CRM) manages, tracking, and communicating with current and future customers. CRM software enables you to log, automate, configure, and analyze deals, contact info, conversations, emails, and much more.

Email marketing

Email marketing and sales are critical for companies of all sizes and styles. It is the most direct method of approaching potential prospects and staying in touch with satisfied current customers. As a result, successful email marketing and selling necessitate the use of high-quality email tools.

There are some different forms of email techniques that can be used. Depending on the target demographic, products/services, and where the recipient is in the sales cycle, each involves intelligent formatting, copywriting, design, and strategies. Good email software collects data on the emails you send, allowing you to optimize various metrics.

Social Media

Social media marketing is one of the most effective types of marketing, especially for small niche businesses. However, it can be a significant time drain and diversion, especially for solo professionals who work both a side hustle and a full-time job. It's almost tricky – and potentially a flawed idea – to update social media sites at work, so spare moments are limited to late nights and weekends.

Unfortunately, if you are approaching specific markets, this can be the wrong time. One workaround is to automate and plan notifications to be sent out ahead of time. Certain social media apps enable you to schedule updates on Twitter, Facebook, Instagram, Pinterest, and many other social media platforms.

You can then concentrate on your job while responding to any feedback or experiences when they arise.

Create Your Business Startup Budget

You won't have to buy anything you need to begin all at once, but it's a good idea to create a start-up budget so you can prepare ahead about what you'll need to buy. Check out the U.S. Small Business Administration's video, "Estimating Start-Up Costs," for assistance in determining the start-up costs. Again, for the most accurate picture, speak with entrepreneurs who are doing what you want to do. They may be aware of things that you might not be aware of, such as fluctuating advertising prices.

Take a minimalist approach and postpone big business acquisitions for as long as possible in case you find you don't like your side hustle and want to "pivot" into something else. It might be tempting to purchase a high-end new computer or furnish your home office with brand-new furniture, but saving your startup funds is the best way to keep your options open as your company grows.

How to Get Started with Budgeting

For most small business owners, financial preparation and bookkeeping are time-consuming activities that could be better spent acquiring new customers and improving business models. Still, money and its management, especially budgeting, are critical in deciding how much money needs to be invested in a new venture, how long it will take to see returns, and how long the company will be viable in the long run.

So, what do you do to get started on a solid financial plan?

You should get started on your own with budgeting. In reality, this is an important first step in determining whether or not your side hustle has the potential to become a full-fledged enterprise.

Here's how to get started:

1. Recognize the value of budgeting for your side hustle.

If you consider the income from your freelance work to be merely extra cash, it's time to change your perspective. As an aspiring business owner, you can view this cash flow as funding for your new company rather than spending money on yourself. By budgeting your side hustle money, you can start asking pointed questions and setting tentative targets based on your responses.

Consider the following:

• How much money do I spend per month on overhead? (These are continuing business costs that are not paid to a specific job or service and, as a result, do not produce a profit.)

• How much money do I make per side gig?

• How much of my primary income am I devoting to my side hustle?

• Given the disparity between my side hustle's expenditures and sales, how soon can I expect my company to break even without relying on subsidies from my primary source of income?

• Given all, what business goals are attainable for me in the short term, and what should be postponed until my company has expanded more?

By answering these questions as precisely as possible, you will develop a sense of your new business's financial future as well as a way of keeping yourself on track.

1. Create a rough (but conservative) budget.

Budgeting for your side hustle is similar to budgeting for your personal finances in that it compares how much you spend (expenses) vs. how much you make (revenue).

Often start by defining what you have and what you require. This entails compiling a list of essential equipment or services that your particular business needs to get off the ground, which may include:

- Technology required (computer, smartphone, software licenses)
- A web address (URL registration, web hosting, website developing, etc.)
- Transportation
- Basic marketing costs (brand logo design, business cards and flyers, ads, etc.)

These products are mostly paid for out of pocket. As a result, accounting for them should help you understand how much of your money is leaving the door during the first year of your business's rollout and how much you'll be spending on daily expenditures each month after that.

To stay disciplined and prepared for unexpected situations, always establish a realistic budget in which you slightly underestimate your expected earnings and, conversely, slightly overestimate your expected overhead expenditure.

The key word here is "slightly": don't fiddle with your forecasts too much that they throw off practical calculations. Simply devise a strategy that keeps cash flow on the tighter side, allowing you to deal with unexpected job delays or expenditures, such as equipment repair, without panic.

1. Delegate authority to the experts.

So you've set aside some funds to turn your side hustle into a successful small company, and it's time to get to work.

In addition to your financial strategy, you must now solidify many important factors, including your product, vision, and customer base. As the owner and developer of your new company, you should focus your efforts and resources on the following areas: Refining the quality and value, you provide to your customers and carving out the position your company can occupy in the current market.

Anyone would struggle to fulfill their vision if they were bogged down in relentless bookkeeping, which, in most cases, is unlikely to be their area of expertise anyway. That is why understanding where to hustle for yourself and where to outsource the hustle to more skilled professionals is critical to creating a successful small business.

An experienced bookkeeper will assist you in decluttering and streamlining your financial environment, allowing you to scale your company to the next level. Remember that, just as you are an expert in your field, bookkeepers are specialists in budgeting, financial planning and management, payroll, and tax filings—everything related to your earnings and expenditures!

Tax Planning

If you're not careful enough, the money earned from your side hustle might land you in hot water when it comes to tax season. It just takes one large job or a few new clients to significantly increase your tax bill.

Three ways your side hustle could wreak havoc on your taxes:

• Depending on how hard you worked in the previous year, your tax bill could rise by hundreds (or even thousands) of dollars.

• If your side hustle is good enough, you will be required to pay estimated taxes over the year — and the IRS will slap you with a penalty if you don't.

- And what if the IRS demands evidence that you spent $1,000 on cooking supplies as a business expense? Do you have receipts or bank statements to show how much you spent?

There is a lot to consider, but you must be prepared. Here are some tips to prevent your side hustle from causing problems with your taxes:

Set aside money for self-employment taxes.

Examine your most recent paycheck from your "day job." You'll notice that your employer withholds a portion of your paycheck to pay income taxes before the money reaches your bank account—this is known as federal income tax withholding. Open a separate business savings account and set aside 20–35 percent of all your side hustle money for taxes, regardless of how much or how little you make. That way, you'll have enough money to cover your income taxes as well as any self-employment taxes you might owe on that income. If you do this, you will not be surprised by a large tax bill when tax season arrives.

Determine if you are required to pay estimated taxes.

Our tax structure is based on a "pay-as-you-go" model. That is, the IRS prefers that people pay their taxes over the year rather than in one lump sum. That is why you will have to pay estimated taxes (or quarterly taxes) on the money you earn from your side hustle every quarter during the year.

You should relax if your side hustle only earns a few hundred dollars per year. You actually don't have to be concerned about estimated taxes. Simply keep track of your earnings and file your tax return in the spring, as usual, paying whatever taxes you owe on the extra income.

If you plan to owe more than $1,000 in taxes when you file your tax return, you will generally pay estimated taxes. That is after deducting your federal income tax withholding from the overall tax you anticipate owing this year.

Set up a different checking account for your side business

Setting up a business checking account will allow you to keep your business expenses apart from your personal ones and will assist you in the beginning to establish business credit. You may also want to apply for a company credit card so that you can consolidate all of your expenses and simplify your bookkeeping.

Business credit cards also have bonus programs tied to the types of transactions made by small companies, which you can use to pay for other business purchases. Some small business owners find it useful to set up free accounts on payment sites like Venmo or PayPal to accept fast electronic payments from customers who choose to pay this way. Money received from these sites can be transferred directly to your business bank account.

If you need to accept debit and credit cards, providers such as Clover, PayPal, and Square can help you do so with card readers you can use on your cell phone or tablet. Major invoicing software providers, such as FreshBooks and QuickBooks, allow you to have a payment option on your invoices that allows customers to pay you by credit card or ACH. If your company begins to process a large number of credit card purchases, you can look for a merchant account provider that can set you up with a package that minimizes processing fees.

Make a basic record-keeping method.

For starters, keeping all of your receipts from side hustle-related expenditures in one location will help you find out how much you can claim in business-related deductions. Second, if Uncle Sam ever comes knocking and asks you to check those expenses, you'll have the paper trail to back it up.

Important details to hold for future reference:

- Receipts are a form of receipt.

- Account statements
- Records of commerce
- Types of taxation
- Car costs and mileage

Seek the advice of a tax professional.

Running a side business will make your taxes a little more complex than you're used to. And trying to understand the tax consequences can be difficult. That is why it is important to work with a CPA or a trustworthy tax professional to whom you can turn for advice and tax guidance.

Be sure to look at their qualifications and track record. The IRS recommends that you browse at its Directory of Federal Tax Return Preparers with Credentials and Choose Qualifications. It will assist you in locating preparers in your region who currently hold IRS-recognized professional credentials or hold an Annual Filing Season Program Record of Completion. It would help if you also looked at the specialist associations to which many tax preparers belong.

Four

CHOOSE THE RIGHT SIDE HUSTLE FOR YOU

N ow that you understand the value of getting a side hustle and the amazing effect it can have on your life and career, it's time to find the right one for you.

You may not know it, but there is a whole universe of side hustles available to you right now.

The endless possibilities can be a little daunting, particularly when you consider how many different directions your ability set might take you. So, before I provide you with a long list of ideas to consider, let me walk you through a couple of simple steps to help you find the right side hustle for you.

How to Find the Ideal Side Job for You

Step 1: Make a list of your interests, strengths, and abilities.

Take 10 minutes to write down everything you enjoy doing and are good at. This can vary from artistic abilities or organizational skills to what you do for a living or something you'd like to learn more about.

Step 2: Narrow the list down to one thing you can see yourself devoting a significant amount of time to.

Keep in mind that you are launching a new company on top of your full-time work. That means it has to be something you are enthusiastic about. You must be committed, enthusiastic, and unwavering in your efforts. If you want it to be a full-time job, you'll have to work while you're exhausted, putting in extra hours on top of already hectic days. But you'll know if it's worth the effort.

Step 3: The 10-Person Rule

The following move will assist you in determining if your side hustle is worthwhile. The 10-Person Rule entails reaching out to ten people and asking them some simple questions about their participation in your idea.

Step 4: Begin producing valuable content

It's time to get to work after you've received input from the 10-Person Rule. You don't have to have a product ready to sell right away, and you certainly don't need business cards just yet (or ever?). Simply create a simple website and begin producing helpful material. The audience you cultivate through great content will serve as the base for your company in the future.

Tips to Pick the Right Gig for You

Joining the side hustle bandwagon is a great way to supplement your income and develop as an individual. Here are some tips for choosing the job that best suits your needs and personality.

1. Find a gig that you love.

If you're like most people, you probably work 40 hours a week or more at your primary job, which means you're probably tired and emotionally exhausted by the end of each day. That is why it is important to find a side hustle that you enjoy doing. Pushing yourself to work 10/12 hours a week in addition to your main job would be difficult, so the side work should be something you enjoy doing. Based on this reasoning, an interesting solution might be to turn a hobby, such as animal care, writing, or crafting, into a source of income. This way, the second job won't feel so much like work.

2. Choose something adaptable.

You definitely don't want your side hustle to conflict with your main job, jeopardizing or even damaging your primary source of income. That is why it is beneficial to choose a second job that allows for the most flexibility in schedules and deadlines. Assume you embrace a babysitting position that allows you to arrive at your client's home by 6 p.m. twice a week. So, what if you have to work late at your primary job one of those nights? Suddenly, you find yourself in the midst of a war. If your primary work is highly predictable, you would be better off finding a side hustle with flexible hours, such as doing web design from home and plugging away at the computer whenever it fits your schedule, whether it's 8 p.m. or 3 a.m.

3. Look for a gig with growth potential.

It's not uncommon for a side hustle to become your full-time career. And if you start your side hustle later in life, it might be a good idea to take with you into retirement, where it can act as a source of income while still giving you something interesting to do with your days. That's why it's a good idea to look for a part-time job with growth potential. For example, if you choose to do graphics-related work on the side, that is a career that you will develop as more clients become aware of you. However, if you take a seasonal job at a local restaurant to supplement your income, you can find yourself out of work until things slow down.

4. Find a job that pays well.

Let's be honest: Though you may truly enjoy your side hustle, chances are you're doing it primarily to make money. So, if you're going to work a certain amount of hours per week, you may as well be compensated for them. This isn't to suggest you should do anything you despise just to make more money, but if selling your home-baked cupcakes earns you just $5 an hour after factoring in your time and the cost of ingredients, it may not be worth the effort. (Even though you love baking, you definitely don't need to spend 10 hours a week doing it.) Rather, strive for a nice middle ground: something that will make a significant difference in your finances while still allowing you to learn and have fun.

Common Mistakes to Choosing a Side Hustle Idea

So you've decided to start a side hustle; what's next?

The first step, of course, is to choose something that you like. We've just seen how to do that and what process to follow when choosing. However, I think this is one of the hardest parts for most people to get through. It happens quite often that people make mistakes in choosing the best side hustle for them. This leads many first-timers to abandon their projects before they have even checked their chances of success.

Let's take a look at the most common mistakes people make when selecting a side hustle concept, as well as how you can prevent them.

Doing Something That Everybody Else Is Doing

Consider the following: You're looking to start your side hustle, and you happen to come across the website of an internet wizard who has an excellent business doing freelance writing.

You reason to yourself: That's something I should do. The issue is that you decided to start a side business in a split second based solely on seeing someone else who was thriving and wanting the same success.

This is one of the most common blunders when it comes to choosing a side hustle. You believe you can replicate someone else's performance simply because they have done so. I've discovered that this isn't always the case.

You may be asking yourself : how can I avoid this mistake? Beware that doing research and seeing what other people are doing is a good way to help you come up with ideas for different side businesses you might create, but don't choose something just because someone else has success with it.

Keep a list of those suggestions so you can come back to them later after you've had some time to consider which one is right for you.

Attempting to do something that is outside of your skillset

One of the most common reasons side hustles struggle is choosing something that does not match our skill set. For example, you might believe that a one-on-one coaching business would be a good fit for you.

However, you are oblivious that you are an introvert who dislikes talking to people and finds it mentally and physically exhausting. I know this is true for me, which is why I stick to more passive forms of side hustles rather than something that drains me.

How to Avoid This Mistake: The trick to avoiding this error is concentrating on your strengths rather than weaknesses.

Make a list of the top strengths and weaknesses. Knowing these steps ahead of time will help you avoid falling into this pit and find a side hustle that complements your skills.

Taking on more than you can handle

The next big mistake is taking on a side hustle that needs you to do more work than you can manage.

This was my very first side hustle. Years ago, I entered a network marketing firm that sold life insurance and savings. Although it was enjoyable at first, I soon found myself working nearly 20 to 30 hours a week, which took a significant amount of time away from my family.

On top of that, I wasn't making nearly enough money for the amount of time I was putting in, and in some instances, I was losing money. In the end, I decided it wasn't worth all of my time and effort and moved on.

Do you want to know how to avoid this mistake? Just before you launch your side hustle, figure out how much time you have available in a week to devote to it. Then consider how much time it would take you to handle your side business every week.

For example, I need at least 3 hours a week to build weekly content and send out my weekly newsletter for my side hustle. In addition, I need 5 hours a week to work on my current project list and another 2 hours to deal with miscellaneous tasks ranging from answering emails to updating WordPress plugins. That alone adds up to at least 10 hours a week.

Knowing all of this in advance will save you a lot of time and frustration.

Underestimating the Expenses Involved

Another factor to consider is the expense of running a side hustle. Whatever type of side hustle you have, you will have to invest at some point. For example, if you want to start working in a ride-sharing company, you might believe that all you need to do is download the Uber or Lyft app, and you'll be good to go. False!

To begin, you will almost certainly need to carry additional insurance, as well as cover the extra fuel you will need to drive people around, wear and tear. You might also need to upgrade the vehicle you are driving because both Uber and Lyft require you to have a relatively new vehicle.

If you want to avoid this mistake, do your homework and determine the true costs of the side hustle you want to launch. Make a list of all the expenses. It would help if you also considered how much money it would take to keep your company going regularly. If you know what these costs are, you'll be able to calculate how much you need to earn to keep things running.

Picking More Than One Side Gig

Choosing more than one side hustle has gotten me in trouble more times than I can count. This may be a major problem for you right now. You've selected two ideas that you want, but you can't decide which one to pursue. You decide to do both because you believe you can test them both at the same time. The issue arises when you do not have enough time to devote to both, and you give up out of frustration.

I've been there before, and it can be difficult to narrow down your options.

So, what do you do if you find yourself in this situation?

To begin, you should choose just one idea. I know it's difficult, but choose the one that appeals to you the most. Then I want you to commit to sticking to it for the next six months. If things aren't working out after six months, you have my permission (not that you need it) to pursue another side hustle. However, I guess that this will not occur and that you will have selected the right side hustle for you.

Choosing a Too Wide Niche

Another mistake people make when selecting a side hustle is going too wide. For example, if you want to start a side business building websites for small businesses, this is a good place to start, but millions of small businesses are out there. As Pat Flynn said, "The Riches are in the Niches."

Getting your side hustle done sets you apart from the crowd. People would have difficulty understanding what problem you can solve for them if your side hustle is wide and large.

So, what do you do to stop making this mistake? The only way to ensure that your side hustle is sufficiently niched is to take it down two to three stages. For example, if your side hustle is one-on-one coaching for online business owners, you may want to narrow it down to people who sell digital courses, and you might also narrow it down to people who make less than $10,000 per month but want to earn more than five figures per month.

More customers will see you as the answer to this dilemma and will be more likely to choose you over your rival if you narrow things down a little.

Basing your choice solely on the money

The final mistake is to do something simply because you will make a lot of money off it. A good example of this was when I considered making my private label products and selling them on Amazon. I was following many people in this niche, and they were bragging about earning hundreds of thousands of dollars every month.

This piqued my interest right away, but as time passed, I realized that I didn't care about the product I was selling or what it could do for people, and the money became my sole motivation for this venture. At this point, I realized I didn't want to support people so much as I wanted money.

How to avoid this mistake: First and foremost, understand that almost every side hustle has the potential to make you a decent income, so don't be misled into believing that only those side businesses will earn you a lot of money.

Finally, remember that the most important aspect of any side hustle you start is to provide value to your customers rather than to make money. Earning money is simply a byproduct of producing a high-quality product or service.

Start now!

It's time to have some fun! The only thing left to do once you've identified the ideal side hustle for you is to take action and get started. Side hustling is hard work, but it can be extremely satisfying, particularly if you choose to do work that both fulfills you and pays well.

Five

ONLINE SIDE HUSTLE IDEAS

You can find dozens of sites on the web that offer lists superficially containing hundreds of side hustles without deepening even one. In this book, I have decided to select those that, based on my experience, are the best jobs and to deepen every aspect of them. In this way, you can more easily choose the one that's right for you and start immediately and effectively.

I decided to divide all the jobs that I will present into four main categories.

- Online
- Product related
- Services
- Other

Let's start with online gigs!

English Teacher

Do you believe you have no skills to offer? Consider it again. If you are fluent in English (or any language), you have something that someone else would like to understand. Since English is such a common language, this is where the most opportunities exist. Many people are willing to learn online, and many companies willing to serve as a middleman.

How to Promote Yourself

There are four main things to remember while considering the various ways you'll need to market yourself as an online teacher:

- Are you a college or university graduate?
- Do you have any teaching credentials (TEFL, TESOL, CELTA)?
- What kind of experience do you have to give a prospective online school?
- Are you a native English speaker, or do you speak English as a second language?

Missing one or two of the above properties does not disqualify you from teaching online English or any other form of ESL, for that matter. These are simply excellent methods for marketing yourself and obtaining the best job possible, in the location you want, and at the best possible price! So, if you have them, show them off.

Relevant university degrees can get you much more easily into an online English school than without. However, there have been several cases where teachers have been recruited with only an associate's degree or less. There are no governing TEFL associations, so there are no standards. It varies according to the needs of each educational organization. Your suitability for any teaching position will be determined by how well you present yourself, your credentials, and your strengths.

TEFL certificates are another aspect of online English teaching that is preferred but not needed. There are thousands of online English teachers around the world who have decades of experience but no certification. It's an excellent way to hone your skills as an ESL instructor if you have the time and resources, but experience trumps every piece of paper. Many schools will state that "TEFL qualification is required" in their job listings, but this does not deter you from applying.

Native English speakers are in high demand, especially in online English teaching. A simple search would reveal thousands of non-native speakers populating the "Our Teachers" pages spread across the Internet. If you are a native English speaker, use it to your advantage in marketing. If you are a non-native English speaker, posting TOEFL or TOEIC test results will significantly increase your marketability!

Consider yourself a commodity. Make a list of any skills you have that could be applicable to online English teaching and include them on your resume. Marketing is a critical component of online English teaching, and it may be the single most significant factor in determining whether or not you will be hired.

Join a School or Fly Solo

Choosing whether to attend a school or seek out students privately is also a critical element of online English teaching to remember.

Each choice has distinct advantages and disadvantages, but no one says you can't do both if you have the time. Many teachers alternate between loving the online English school life and moonlighting and filling in everyday time gaps as opportunities arise.

Teaching for an online school is an excellent way to secure flexible teaching positions within days or weeks of being employed. There are already students in the online English schools you're searching for. You will almost certainly be given some structure, preparation, or worksheets and models to work with. Teaching for an online school will also provide you with a one-of-a-kind support network of administrators and other online English teachers. This can be useful if you become ill, have an emergency, or just want to take a break.

Flying solo in the world of online English teaching can be just as rewarding, entertaining, and exciting if you're an expert at finding your student base. The majority of people who are effective at finding students on their own are natural extroverts. If you live in Brazil and like to go out and enjoy the nightlife, networking would be better than advertising. You'll be your own boss, which means you'll have boss issues. You'll need to plan, invoice, and collect payments from your students, which takes time and can be difficult. You'll just have to find out how to pay your taxes, which can be difficult for some.

Identifying Your Niche

Finding your niche or special position in online English teaching is critical to your overall success and ability to attract students. This normally appears after you've spent some time teaching and getting acquainted with the online format. In the absence of a classroom, you may find yourself awkwardly looking into a blank Skype screen, urgently attempting to direct your student toward the lesson goals and goal.

A niche is your personality coupled with the areas of ESL in which you excel. Yes, online teachers sometimes have to teach various ESL skills depending on the student for that hour, but you'll notice that more and more students gravitate toward one or two basic ESL areas you teach. These may be business classes, casual talks, simple textbooks, professional presentations, technical English, science English, legal English, or something similar.

It is critical to concentrate on finding and marketing your niche, whether through social media, commercials, or even student word of mouth. Your niche and position in online English teaching will make you famous with students, which will result in more lessons, money, and valuable experience.

Getting Paid

You're teaching, working hard, and creating high-quality lesson plans that are helping you become the well-known online English teacher you've always wanted to be. But it's now time to get paid! Getting paid can be a challenging aspect of teaching English online, and it is an aspect that most teachers ignore until the time comes to go to the ATM.

If you're teaching for an online school, you can settle on a salary that you're comfortable accepting before signing any contracts. A variety of variables influences this figure. Consider the following benefits of working online that could be worth taking a pay cut for:

- no travel time or cost,
- no out-of-pocket expenses for lunch,
- and no need to buy new clothes regularly.

Consider the extra expenses you would incur as a result of this line of work:

- high-speed internet,
- higher total utility costs,
- and extra job time "off the clock" for lesson planning.

Check out what other teachers are charging on work searching websites for online English teachers if you're teaching privately. The hourly rate you can charge will vary depending on the region.

Another critical factor to consider is the consistency and credibility of the online school you wish to work with. Perform your due diligence to ensure that they pay what they pledge. Typically, any online English school that has wronged a teacher or teachers will face a torrent of negative online blogging, Facebook messages, and other forms of destruction. If you're working on your own, always accept payment in advance if possible. This is a common activity that will put the mind at ease. In any case, make sure to plan ahead of time for your tax situation. If your online school does not subtract taxes from your salary and does not provide you with official tax documents, you may need to learn how to file as a self-employed individual.

One piece of advice for aspiring online teachers: Set up a Paypal, Wise or Payoneer account online to collect payments whether you work from a school or privately teach online. These accounts will keep your banking details safe and enable students to make payments from anywhere in the world.

Finding Online English Teaching Jobs

There is only one way to look for an online English school where you want to teach: SEARCH!

You could spend an entire day surfing the web and just get three or four resumes out the door. Another common problem when looking for an online English school is a lack of response or the length of time it takes to hear back. Don't let it demotivate you. Continue to apply, and you will be accepted into the online English school of your choice.

Keep in mind that not all online English schools are created equal, and many of their teacher requirements differ significantly. Again, the more research you conduct, the better. Before you accept any role, make sure you understand precisely what the school expects of you. Some schools need comprehensive reports, dealing with students and rescheduling problems, regular or weekly meetings, and asking teachers to develop large lesson plans, all of which would most likely not be compensated for.

There are a few excellent websites where you can start your quest and study online schools. Despite all of its coverage, both positive and negative, Craigslist remains a viable option for finding a successful online English teaching job. Dave's ESL Cafe, Indeed, and Glassdoor are excellent places to start your quest for the best online school for your needs and schedule.

Staying Up to Date With Technology

When it comes to teaching English online, being as technologically savvy as possible is important. Your whole career path is dependent on technology, and if you don't keep up, you will find yourself with fewer options.

You'll need a high-speed Internet connection. A poor Internet connection discourages many students from participating in a particular teacher's class. If you have excellent Internet, with the video and voice quality students expect, you'll be one step ahead of the competition.

You'll need to learn how to use Skype and Zoom. Anything associated with these apps should become your wheelhouse. Most online schools depend on this software as their primary method of instruction. Sharing screens, introducing pupils, and handling contacts are all critical aspects of using Skype.

When addressing technology, another factor to remember is the age of your machine. If your computer is old, noisy, and sluggish due to too many applications, images, songs, and pictures, you should consider upgrading. Online English teachers need quick operating systems to ensure the highest possible level of lesson quality. Your students will be grateful, and you will have a new toy to enjoy! At the very least, you can perform a thorough sweep and clean your hard drive, deleting all unnecessary files and storing the majority of the relevant data on a backup hard drive.

Virtual Assistant

What is a virtual assistant? In short, the role of a virtual assistant is to make someone's life easier.

A VA is an online assistant that offers support to businesses and individuals through the internet and, depending on the work requirements, the phone.

To become a virtual assistant, you do not need any credentials, advanced training, or formal qualification. However, being a VA usually necessitates a particular skill set. The benefit of working as a virtual assistant is that you can provide services based on your expertise, experience, and interests. But, no matter what services you want to provide as a VA, you must be good at them if you want to be effective.

How much do virtual assistants earn?

The amount of money virtual assistants earn per month is determined by their qualifications, experience, and the company for which they work. A novice virtual assistant can earn between $10 and $25 per hour. An experienced VA will earn between $50 and $100 per hour, or much more.

If you work for a virtual assistant organization, they can set your hourly wage. Most VA firms pay between $10 and $20 per hour, depending on the organization. Some of them need you to have prior experience and specific skills to enter them. However, whether you work as a freelance virtual assistant or start your own virtual assistant company, you have complete control over how much you charge for your services.

You may not earn as much money as an experienced VA who has been in business for a while if you are just starting out as a VA. However, if you specialize in a specific field, such as graphic design, SEO, or WordPress services, you can charge much higher rates even if you have just started this job.

How do you start a side hustle as a virtual assistant?

So, do you want to be a virtual assistant to supplement your income while working full-time? You can become a VA if you have some simple skills such as typing, data entry, email management, and so on, but you may need to learn a few sought-after skills to stand out from the crowd.

If you want to work as a virtual assistant to supplement your income, here's what you'll need to get started.

- Develop the skills required to work as a virtual assistant

To become a virtual assistant, you must have some fundamental skills. If you want to begin a VA career, you must have the following basic skills:

- Computer skills

- Organizational skills

- Attention skills

- Communication skills

- Typing skills

- Project management skills

If you have these abilities, you can start today. If you lack them, a good virtual assistant course will teach you everything you need to learn about beginning a virtual assistant side hustle.

- Take a virtual assistant training course

If you are a total novice, you may want to enroll in an online virtual assistant course to learn everything you need to know about this side job. There are many online courses, but I suggest conducting your research to find the best VA course for you.

After taking a good course, you will have completely mastered all the facts, tips and tricks needed to start a virtual assistant (side) business. Completing a course can also help you establish credibility with potential clients.

Determine the services you want to provide as a VA

While the type of work you do as a virtual assistant varies and is determined by factors such as your skillset, niche, preferences, previous occupation, and even place – some services are more in demand than others. Offering a variety of services eliminates the need for your clients to outsource to several freelancers, making their lives simpler and you a more appealing choice.

Here is a list of the top services that people pay for that virtual assistants provide:

Customer Care

Customer care is one of the most common tasks that a virtual assistant can assist with. Keeping customers happy is critical for any company that wants to prosper – but it takes a considerable amount of time. And business owners don't have too much time on their hands, which is why they recruit and pay awesome people like you to make their lives easier.

As a virtual assistant, you may do the following customer service tasks:

- Responding to consumer inquiries
- Real-time assistance to customers (e.g., Live Chat)
- Order processing
- Shipment administration
- Payment chasing
- Keeping accurate records

Finance Administration

Many people need assistance in staying on top of their businesses, whether personal finances, company finances, or both. If you have any experience in this field and are good with numbers, you may provide your clients with financial management services such as:

- Tax preparation
- Taking care of retirement funds
- Debt repayment tracking
- Invoice development, transmission, and tracking
- Payment processing
- Making a profit and loss statement
- Bookkeeping

Administrative Assistance

Admin functions are relatively simple – and are most likely associated with virtual assistant roles. Administrative assistance can include:

- Making appointments and phone calls
- Keeping track of the schedule/calendar
- Voicemail monitoring
- Organizing transportation
- Reports/PDF documents development
- Email, internal communication, and so on.
- Creating PowerPoint presentations
- Organizing files (e.g., DropBox, Google Drive, etc.)
- Creating spreadsheets and entering data

Social Media Administration

It's not just spreadsheets and delivery orders for a virtual assistant! Companies can recruit you if you already know (or are eager to learn) how to handle social media accounts.

Being involved in social media as a company is critical today – but developing a strong social media presence, once again, necessitates a significant time commitment and specialized expertise. Therefore, business owners can outsource social media management tasks to people who are more knowledgeable than them.

Tasks associated with social media management can include:

- Using social media sites to post (e.g., Facebook, Instagram)
- Updating profiles regularly
- Responding to comments to maintain interaction
- Creating SM campaign ideas – and putting them into action
- Using social media to reach out to new potential customers
- Keeping up to date on the promotional rules for each platform
- Understanding social SEO and using it to maximize your posts

Content Development

Businesses also need quality content to create and sustain interaction with their audiences. Offering content development services can put you ahead of other virtual assistants.

Here are a few content creation services you might provide:

- Blog post creation and formatting
- Editing and proofreading
- Keyword analysis
- Creating SEO-friendly posts
- Image sourcing and editing
- Researching and recommending subjects
- Producing infographics
- Creating engaging content from business data
- Including affiliate hyperlinks
- Scheduling post to publish

Website/Blog Administration

Many companies often use digital assistants to handle their websites and/or blog. So, if you're familiar with WordPress, this might be a great service to add to your VA kit. Running your own blog will teach you everything you need to know, and you can even consider monetizing it to create an additional source of income.

Here are a few examples of website/blog management tasks you may be assigned for your client:

- Fixing broken links
- Setting redirects
- Delete old, out-of-date, or unwanted pages and posts
- Comment moderation and response

- Installing and updating plug-ins
- Improving the SEO of the website
- Developing a thorough understanding of the blog's results (KPIs)
- Reporting on current trends and topics
- Tracking metrics (e.g., Google Analytics or other tools)

Internet Marketing

With 85 percent of the US population now online (and the number of internet users continues to rise!), most companies must do everything possible to optimize the effectiveness of their online marketing. Any company's primary aim is to connect with their target audience – assuming they want to sell their product or service.

If you have expertise in the area of online marketing, you would be extremely useful as a virtual assistant. Here is a list of some services you might provide:

- Creating Search Engine Optimized Landing Pages
- Organizing webinars (and providing tech support, if needed)
- Developing sales pages
- Managing deals and promotions
- Creating brochures and flyers
- Managing the introduction of new products
- Planning paid advertisement campaigns
- Measuring the impact of ads

Email Marketing

Although some advertisers claim that email marketing is dead, statistics show that this is not the case. Not only are there more than 5.6 billion active email accounts worldwide, but the United States is expected to spend $390 million on email ads in 2021.

Here are some email marketing services you might provide to your customers:

- Creating email templates
- Email scheduling
- Creating and distributing newsletters
- Keeping track of the subscriber list
- Product launch management
- Monitoring the efficacy of email marketing campaigns (e.g., click-throughs, conversion, unsubscribes, etc.)

Email Administration

Nobody enjoys seeing thousands of unanswered emails in their inbox. To be honest, it gets to the point that I'm tempted to unintentionally click "archive everything" – and pretend I never got them.

But it is not a wise decision. Instead, why not employ someone to manage your inbox? That is exactly what people can employ a virtual assistant to assist them with. Email management tasks can include:

- Creating responses (e.g., to common questions)
- Mark relevant emails as important
- Unsubscribing from unsolicited promotional material
- Following up on critical emails that were sent
- Spam management (e.g., creating junk mail filters)
- Email archiving

Increasing Business Exposure

Building partnerships and increasing visibility are essential for any company that wishes to develop a sustainable brand. And, while there are numerous ways to increase a company's exposure, they are incredibly time-consuming – which is why businesses can employ a virtual assistant to handle it. You may provide a variety of outreach VA programs, such as:

- Engaging in discussions with bloggers
- Participating in appropriate forums
- Making contact with influencers and exploring potential partnerships
- Creating Leads
- Taking care of affiliate programs
- Creating and distributing press releases
- Contacting sponsors or advertisers

Choose who you want to collaborate with

If you've determined what services you'd like to provide, you'll need to figure out what kind of companies you'd like to partner with. Determine the types of businesses that might benefit from your services and then search for positions advertised by these companies online. You may also reach out to any of these companies to see if they need your services.

If you provide transcription services, you can concentrate your efforts on applying for VA jobs that require transcription skills. You can collaborate with bloggers if you have writing and proofreading skills.

Set your working hours

The great thing about working as a virtual assistant is that you can set your own hours, particularly if you work freelance. If you are currently employed, you must determine your working hours for your VA side hustle. Determine how many hours and days you will devote to your VA side hustle. You must notify potential clients when you cannot function, and they do not expect you to communicate with them.

Set your pricing

When it comes to creating a virtual assistant side hustle, determining the pricing for your VA services is critical. When you first begin as a virtual assistant, determining how much to charge for your services can be challenging.

As of the time of publication, the average hourly wage for a virtual assistant in the United States was $19.00 per hour, according to ZipRecruiter. However, most inexperienced VAs charge between $10 and $25 per hour or more.

Depending on the job, you can also charge a flat rate for some services. Simply make sure to charge a fair hourly rate or a flat fee for your services. It might be tempting to set your rates lower than those of other new virtual assistants to attract prospective customers, but you should not set your rates too low even if you are a beginner VA. If you're having trouble pricing your services, check out the prices other people in the same niche have set for that service; plus that, I advise you to set a lower price at the beginning as a marketing strategy in order to find more clients where you are making the first steps towards building your business.

Make a name for yourself as a VA

Working as a virtual assistant online necessitates marketing your services online. Creating a website and social media accounts is the perfect way to advertise yourself as a virtual assistant online.

Inform your network that you are now providing virtual assistant services. Promote your services on social media websites such as Facebook, Twitter, Instagram, and LinkedIn by posting your VA profile on different pages, as well as sharing your website. You could get your first client from someone you know. If you get clients through your network, they can refer you to others they know.

When you first start out, you should consider doing small jobs to develop your VA side hustle. After completing a few jobs successfully, ask your clients for testimonials to feature on your website so that potential clients can see what sets you apart from other VAs.

How to Get a Job as a VA

Clients can be found in a variety of ways. To find work as a VA, you can ask family and friends for recommendations, connect with potential employers on social media, enter virtual assistant companies online, answer job ads, or sign up for freelance sites.

If you're curious, "Where will I find virtual assistant jobs?" you have two options: work for a VA company as an employee, or work directly for clients as a freelance virtual assistant.

In the first case, you will not be able to set your prices for your services. Although the pay isn't as good as you'd want it to be and you won't have much control of your work hours if you work for a virtual assistant company, it is easier to find clients this way.

As a freelancer, you can find VA jobs on many websites, such as:

- Fiverr
- Upwork
- Freelancer
- PersonsPerHour
- FlexJobs
- Outsourcely
- Indeed

In addition to the websites listed above, check through social media and contact local businesses to find clients for your VA side hustle.

Writing

I was just a year out of high school when I was asked to write professionally for a living. A local company needed a blogger, and one of my football teammates generously recommended me for the role. Writing was my unintentional side hustle for many years. Until, of course, it became my full-time career.

If there is one writing secret I had to discover for myself, it is this: the demand for good writers far exceeds the supply. If you are a professional writer willing to assist companies, I can tell you from personal experience that there is a high demand for your time and talent.

What you need to know before you start

Various Writing Styles

The first point I'd like to make is that there are many ways of writing. When it comes to writing, there are a plethora of different places to get your start.

You are not required to write only blog material, for example. Blog content is nice and all, and there's a lot of it out there to be posted. There are a lot of people who want that kind of content. However, you might be more interested in doing something like proofreading, just to give you an idea.

Fiverr is a good place to start looking. Simply, you can go there and get a lot of different ideas. To begin, you have blogs, blog posts, resume, cover letters, technical writing, translation, creative writing, analysis and summaries, sales copy, press releases, transcripts, legal writing, proofreading, beta reading, speech writing, development, product descriptions, book and e-book writing, scriptwriting, and website material.

And the list continues indefinitely. It means that there are numerous ways to supplement your income as a freelance writer through your company. When you're just starting out, there are several options.

Skill Level

Another point I'd like to bring up is skill level. The level of expertise is critical. If you don't have writing experience, you're probably not going to be the best when you first start out. Perhaps you were in college, and you have a background in freelance writing or something similar. This will be more beneficial to you as an individual, but you'll have to learn many things quickly if you're just getting started. So the more you improve your writing skills, the faster you will end up making more money as a result.

If I had to begin a writing side gig from scratch today, with no writing samples or marketing experience, this is where I'd start.

Create a blog for a local company

One of my first continuing writing gigs since becoming a full-time freelancer was writing 1–2 blogs per week for a local company. They charged me $35 per hour, which amounted to hundreds (sometimes thousands) of dollars per month. Daily blogging is also one of the easiest ways to generate a steady writing income without constantly pitching new customers.

Client-finding advice

Participate in blogs such as Upwork or Thumbtack. These places helped me pull in tens of thousands of dollars in new writing clients during my first few years of freelancing. Every day, new companies use freelance blogs to find consistent bloggers. You could be their next recruit.

Write for people in your network as ghostwriters

Simply put, ghostwriting is the use of your writing skills to assist someone else in communicating their stories and ideas — under their name. You write in their voice. Many actors, politicians, athletes, and business executives hire ghostwriters to assist them with their publishing. You just need to get your name in front of them.

Client-finding advice

Connect to your network. You're probably aware of business owners or influencers who regularly need material to be published under their names. Request that you write their next LinkedIn report, blog post, or Instagram post. Since they're in your network, you've most likely already bridged the trust gap. You just need to make the deal.

Write whitepapers and ebooks

Brush up on your long-form writing skills. Many businesses, especially those that sell to other businesses (known as B2B, or business-to-business), have an ongoing need to create long-form tools such as ebooks, whitepapers, and various other guides. These tools assist prospective consumers in comprehending the company's product or business. If you have a talent for writing entertaining content at length and simplifying technical subjects, this might be your ticket to consistent writing work.

Client-finding advice

Navigate to the LinkedIn search bar. Fill in the blanks with a word you believe someone would use if they needed to employ a freelance copywriter. Something along the lines of "looking for a freelance copywriter" or "hiring an ebook writer." When you have your results, filter them by Content and Date (rather than Relevance) to get the most recent requests. Then, simply answer to everyone who is looking for your expertise.

Write case studies for companies that provide services

Are you at ease performing brief interviews? You may specialize in writing case studies for local service companies. Every service company will benefit from getting a case study or two on their website. The problem is that many business owners don't have time (or don't know where to begin) to draft one. That is your ticket to starting a profitable writing side hustle.

Client-finding advice

One of the most popular methods of obtaining freelance writing clients is cold pitching. The catch is that it's just a numbers game. You must devote time to pitching your services to hundreds of companies. As a general rule, demonstrate that you've done your homework and understand the person to whom you're pitching. A lot of cold pitching is achieved without any personalization, which guarantees that you will be overlooked. Instead, be friendly and approachable. Send an email to small service businesses in your region. Inquire whether they need case studies to highlight their best work.

Produce amazing social media content

One of the keys to social media success is consistency. To be honest, many small business owners don't have the time to create endless content on their own, let alone react to every comment and direct message. If you can write quick, catchy social media posts, thousands of companies will gladly hand over control of all their social networks to you.

Client-finding advice

Look online for marketing and design firms in your area. (Once again, being local can be advantageous here.) If an organization you find does not mention social media marketing and management as a service, introduce yourself via email. Suggest yourself as someone to whom the agency should refer potential social media work. Many agencies actually refuse clients who request work that they do not have. However, it looks easier on them if they have anyone to talk to instead. In this strategy, you make the organization appear trustworthy while also building a powerful referral network.

Parting thoughts

Writing is a self-contained marketing engine. The more you write and the more individuals and companies you write about, the easier it will be to find your next project. Good writing attracts potential writing jobs.

The most difficult part is simply getting started. If you can get over the hurdle — ideally by using some of the tips above — you'll be well on your way to making a profitable writing side hustle.

Where to Look for Freelance Writing Jobs

Upwork

In 2015, oDesk and Elance, two of the biggest freelance work sites, merged. As a result, Upwork now has over 12 million freelancers, 5 million employers, and 3 million freelance job listings per year.

This marketplace offers a wide range of freelance work, and many freelance writing jobs are available, ranging from blogging to resume writing, website copywriting to technical documentation. They have short-term contracts, long-term contracts, hourly jobs, and project-based compensation.

Suppose you're just starting out as a freelance writer. In that case, you'll have an uphill battle to develop a portfolio and a reputation on the web (experienced freelancers can just add their existing portfolio items to get jobs and reviews more quickly). However, the site's job diversity ensures that you'll still be able to find employment if you're willing to put in the effort to submit proposals.

The most significant disadvantage is the 20% premium Upwork costs for the first $500 you earn from every customer. You may also pay up to $0.90 for each proposal for which you were not expressly invited to apply. As a result, if you're just starting out, you can have to pay-to-play in order to construct your portfolio.

FlexJobs

FlexJobs is an online career platform that caters to both freelancers and people looking for flexible full-time work.

What is the main difference with competitors? FlexJobs screens and verifies all of their jobs to ensure that there are no scams or low-paying gigs. This is ideal for more seasoned freelance authors because it saves time filtering through garbage. However, if you're just starting out and need to develop a portfolio, you'll have a more difficult time finding work. With their personalized career hunt, FlexJobs also makes it easy to find the ideal job for you.

This allows you to narrow down the job categories (there are many types of "writing" jobs available), your desired work schedule, experience level, and so on, so you can see and apply for only the jobs that interest you.

To gain access to the freelance writing jobs on FlexJobs, you must first sign up for a subscription.

Textbroker

Textbroker is a freelance writing platform that functions similarly to a large-scale agency.

They screen freelance writers for accuracy before giving you access to the hundreds of product descriptions, press releases, web copy, blogs, and other writing jobs posted by their customers (they claim they deliver on over 100,000 content orders a month).

Signing up as a writer is absolutely free; all you have to do is check your US citizenship and submit a writing sample. They'll award you a ranking of 2-5 stars, and you'll be off to the races! You can get work by entering an open order (first come, first served), which is convenient because you don't have to "sold" a client on hiring you first.

You can also be put on a team of other writers to be employed together, or clients can give you work directly – all while Textbroker manages payments and project workflows. This is perfect for beginners, but more seasoned writers will want to look elsewhere because of the low pay.

Problogger

With the ProBlogger job board, you know two things: the jobs are probably solid, and they will most likely be blogging-related.

When you dig deeper, you'll discover that this is mostly true, though there are a few copywriting jobs thrown in for good measure. The board itself is straightforward – it is free to browse and apply for writing work.

There is no need to sign up; simply find a position that interests you and apply. However, if you like, you can join the Candidate dashboard (for free) to add your resume, manage applications, and receive career notifications.

One disadvantage is that there aren't many positions left. When I was searching, I found 2-6 jobs a day, but this is a well-known blogosphere platform, so it's a reasonably competitive place. Furthermore, the positions aren't screened, so you'll have to do your own research (though they have tips for that right in the applications).

Freelancer.com

Freelancer.com is a similar online career platform to Upwork. That is, you can build a profile, apply for work, be hired and paid via their website, and then rinse and repeat.

There are thousands of jobs available (including online writing jobs), both by hours and at a fixed project rate.

Freelancer also provides a third "Contest" option in which clients post their work requirements, freelancers create the requested material, and the client selects and pays for their favorite(s).

This might not be so appealing for experienced freelancers who can rely on their current profiles, testimonials, and sales skills. However, it is ideal for new freelance writers because it allows you to develop your portfolio while still having a chance to get paid – without requiring a lot of experience!

The drawbacks are in the fees: after your first eight bids per month, you'll have to pay to apply to work. You'll also have to pay a 10% commission on all hours and project costs you bill through them.

Freelance Writing

The FreelanceWriting.com job board, established in 1997, features journalism, material, copywriting, and blogging gigs from all over the web, including Indeed, Craigslist, and BloggingPro!

There is no need to sign up; simply search their carefully curated list of available jobs and filter by source, skills required, location (including remote freelance writing jobs), keyword, and date added. Another cool feature of Freelance Writing's website is a compilation of writing competitions from around the web.

These are excellent for beginners who want to learn how to get started in freelance writing because you can create your portfolio by creating pieces for these contents. You could even win and raise some real money!

At the end of the day, the only real disadvantage can be found on almost every writing work board: there is no organized procedure for applying, being hired, and getting paid.

Contena

Contena is a high-end freelance writing website aspiring to be more than just "another work board." It's one of my top picks for freelance writing websites.

For starters, they have a "writing career finder" that automatically gathers the best freelance writing gigs from across the world. Then you can browse and filter through them to find the best opportunities, whether it's a $10,000 per month full-time eBook writing job or a one-time blog post in the sports niche.

That saves you a lot of time from having to go to a bunch of different job search sites.

However, their Alerts notifications, which are sent to your inbox regularly, save you even more time by displaying only the jobs that suit your requirements, such as rates and niche. Other features that contribute to this being one of the best freelance writing websites for both beginners and veterans include:

Courses – learn how to start freelance writing on the weekend and expand after that.

Coaching – get expert advice on how to advance your freelance writing career.

Pro Prices – displays the average rates that writers receive, allowing you to price your work accordingly.

Publish – allows you to build your portfolio using their beautiful and simple software.

Even though you must apply and pay for their platform, the work they produce is of such high quality that it easily pays for itself.

Constant Content

Constant Content is a content development service that has assisted over 50,000 companies in finding freelance authors to produce a variety of web content, including social media articles, product profiles, blog posts, and ebooks.

To apply for freelance writing jobs, you must first build a profile to highlight your experience and skills, then take a quiz and submit a 100-250 word sample.

If you are accepted, you will be able to apply to projects that interest you, work independently or as part of a team, and develop a reputation that will lead to clients asking to work with you! Overall, this is an excellent place to begin and establish a baseline amount of work for yourself.

However, Constant Content does not encourage you to contact the companies with which you work outside of their website. As a result, you will be unable to develop your client relationships to extend your position or obtain referrals.

Podcasting

Podcasting has quickly become one of the most widely and commonly consumed types of media on the internet. Someone in any possible niche seems to be making a podcast about something they are interested in. With the concurrent, exponential growth of online video and other types of shared online media, the popularity of podcasts begs some questions for today's entrepreneurs, business owners, and side hustlers.

Why are podcasts so popular?

Several factors have led to the unmistakable development of the podcast format. The first one is that any user can find a podcast regarding any topic of his interest. Whether it's personal development, business and economics, art, culture, or the most obscure hobby, there's bound to be a podcast for it.

Furthermore, the format is simple to consume. Text and video require a consumer's undivided attention. Podcasts are ideal for listening to while driving, in the background on headphones at work, while preparing dinner, or catching up on laundry over the weekend. The format is extremely open, and since it allows consumers to multitask while listening, they can listen to a podcast at any time.

What Are the Benefits?

Podcasting broadens a brand's or business's scope and fosters loyalty among a target audience. It enables brands and businesses to publish their content in a common, widely consumed long-form media format to increase their overall market exposure.

Consumers who regularly listen to podcasts develop a strong sense of loyalty at a rapid pace. After a few hours of listening to the same podcast, they develop a sense of familiarity and comfort with the individual or people who run the show. Making them much more likely to purchase your product or service in the future.

Why Should More People Begin Podcasting?

Individuals, brands, companies, side hustlers, and entrepreneurs can use podcasting to express their passion and create communities with a specific audience. It enables them to increase overall exposure in a niche market and create user, fan, and customer loyalty at a pace unrivaled by other digital advertising formats. With the ease of listeners being able to listen to a podcast at any time and from any place, the benefits of making a podcast far outweigh any disadvantages.

If you want to start your podcast, please read the following hints carefully.

Find Out Your Idea

Creating a podcast, like every other side hustle, starts with an idea. A common mistake is to create a podcast that is too general or broad. On the other hand, if you appeal to a particular audience, the people who will listen to your podcast will fall in love with it right away. Niching down is now the most successful way to stand out from the crowd and increase the chances of your show's success.

Finding a niche entails narrowing down the podcast subject to appeal to a particular audience. Essentially, you don't want a podcast that is so broad that no one knows what it's about or who it's about. A podcast about the past of the women's rights movement in the United States, for example, is much more specialized than a general history podcast. It has a narrow emphasis and therefore appeals to a small group of people.

I understand how easy it is to fall into the pit of attempting to cater to the broadest possible audience. However, this is not the only way to gain a following. There are so many podcasts out there these days that you will almost certainly face a lot of competition regardless of your subject. So you must find a way to distinguish yourself. The simplest way to do this is to tailor your podcast to a specific type of audience.

So, how can you figure out what your niche is? You must choose a narrow subject to entice listeners while remaining wide enough to allow you to say a lot about it. If you don't know where to begin, this can be difficult. So here are some pointers to help you along the way.

Write down a general list

If you're just getting started with your podcast subject, you may want to start with brainstorming. List anything, and all that comes to mind - no idea is too large or too small at the moment. Don't be concerned about whether your subject is sufficiently niche at this point; you can narrow it down later. If you're having trouble coming up with ideas, consider the following:

- What are your interests and hobbies?
- What are you comfortable talking about for an extended time?
- What is it that you are most concerned about?
- What do you know a lot about?
- What is it that people come to you for advice on?

Feel free to look at what podcasts are already available and draw inspiration from them.

Choose your favorites and divide them into niches

Now that you have a list of subjects pick the ones that seem to be the most promising. Which ones pique your interest the most? Which ones do you already see a few episodes of?

After you've determined your favorite subjects, it's time to segment them into niches. Consider subtopics inside your concept - the more descriptive, the better. Also, consider if you can approach the subject from a novel angle. Perhaps you have specific experiences or skills that allow you to see things from a different perspective. A podcast about Japanese history from someone who has lived in Japan for a few years, or a podcast about women's rights from someone who has real activism experience, are much more appealing because they are tailored to the host. Consider what unique perspectives you can add to your podcast that no one else can. That is what will set your show apart.

Think about what makes you unique

If you're still having trouble narrowing down your subjects, you might find it useful to do some brainstorming about yourself. Yes, you are right. Spend some time thinking about what sets you apart from the crowd before creating a podcast about your subject.

You do not, however, need a Ph.D. to have a niche. Something special about you and your previous experience will provide you with a new angle to play on. Whatever it is, the more specific your niche is to you as the host, the better - it gives people a reason to listen to your show over those on the same subject.

You can always diversify later

If you're concerned that your niche is too narrow, remember that it's not supposed to be a prison. It is intended to assist you rather than to limit you unnecessarily. As a result, you can still broaden or narrow your focus later on. After you've played around with your subject a bit, you'll probably have a better understanding of what you have to offer, and you can adjust your niche accordingly.

If you've developed a loyal following, you can afford to extend the scope of your podcast. If you already have a following, they won't mind if you stray from the subject every now and then. However, if you're still trying to develop your audience, having a particular niche will help draw people in from the start. As a result, make sure your podcast is focused enough to begin with.

Find and fill your niche

Finding a niche is the simplest way to stand out from the crowd and get people to appreciate your podcast when they see it. All you have to do is decide what you can add to a podcast that is exclusive to others. That can come from anywhere - whether you have personal experience with the subject, a unique perspective to give, or an interest in a specific subtopic.

Your niche does not have to be a shackle; you can always play around with it before finding one that works for you. However, knowing what it is from the start will help you create an audience. When your target audience sees your performance in the crowd, they will pause and believe it was made just for them.

How to Make Money from Your Podcast

While it may be tempting to believe that podcasting is a fast way to make money, the fact is that no podcast monetization plan can succeed if you don't have a listener base. Your priority should be to create content that people love — content that encourages them to invite you into their lives. Any monetization plan will fail unless you first build an audience.

You should adopt monetization techniques once you have an audience. Essentially, there are two types of podcast monetization strategies: direct and indirect. Direct monetization entails selling the podcast itself — we'll go over how to do this. In comparison, indirect monetization entails using the podcast to sell other items. Whatever the monetization tactics are, keep in mind that your primary duty is to your audience. No monetization plan would be worth the effort unless you listen to them and keep them entertained first.

Now, let's get into the specifics and talk about podcast monetization strategies.

Request donations from your audience

This isn't going to provide you with much of a revenue source on its own, but it can be used in combination with more lucrative tactics to help you raise money from your podcast. If you host your podcast on your website — which you can do pretty cheaply with services like SoundCloud and Squarespace — you can still add a PayPal donation button and encourage people to donate.

To successfully monetize your podcast, you'll need to do much more than simply solicit donations. However, it is something you can begin doing right away and without much difficulty.

Charge a fee for podcast subscriptions

If people have gotten into the habit of consuming your material, the next move is to start charging them for it. Patreon and Podia, for example, allow you to set up a subscription system where people pay to listen to your podcast. Many podcasters use Patreon to create different membership rates, giving subscribers growing levels of content and other benefits.

Now, if you put all of your content behind a paywall and reserve it for paying subscribers, you may have difficulty extending your reach and attracting new listeners who aren't already familiar with you. That is why it is beneficial to study what other podcasters have done to overcome this problem.

You can now play with your free-to-paid content ratio, but it's usually a good idea to leave a portion of your podcast episodes behind your paywall to draw more casual listeners. Nevertheless, monetizing your back catalog is a viable choice after you've been podcasting for a while.

Sell merchandise

Famous podcasters sometimes do this. You will sell branded products (t-shirts, laptop stickers, mugs, etc.) to higher-tier subscribers in addition to podcast access. You can also charge a fee for access to online classes, exclusive interviews, and other material that increases demand for your product (that would be you).

If your podcast covers a subject on which you are an expert, you can also offer your consulting services. The point is, once your podcast has grown in popularity to the point that you and your brand are valuable, it might be time to capitalize on that popularity.

Of course, this will not pay off while you are just starting out. You can't use your brand to drive sales if customers aren't familiar with it.

Turn old content into a book and sell it

When you are making money by selling new content, you can also monetize your existing content. You can repackage and resell your older content in new formats.

If you've done a range of podcasts on a specific subject in the past and you like them, you could transcribe them (either entirely or selectively), add material as you see fit, and compile it all into a book that you could sell on Amazon. Remember to promote your book on your podcast!

Make your podcasts available on YouTube

YouTube makes it easy to publish and monetize videos, so you can earn money by posting podcast episodes to YouTube with a little video editing. You could simply use a static picture as your video and play the episode audio alongside it, or you could film yourself while recording the podcast.

You could try breaking up an episode into shorter segments for easier digestibility on YouTube. You can get several pieces of YouTube content from a single podcast episode this way.

Affiliate Marketing

We've spoken about how you can make money by selling your podcast-related stuff. Let's look at how you can make money selling things that aren't your own. Affiliate marketing is one way to do this.

There are several affiliate programs that you can simply join; you can begin earning money as soon as people sign up through your affiliate connection. These programs do not need approval from the organization, and these ties will continue to earn you money for months or even years as long as the program is active. You may also want to start a blog with details about the items you list on your show.

The goods you sell should be linked to what you do and what you actually use when doing your podcast — otherwise, you risk losing credibility with your audience. You can also report your affiliate relationships at this stage. Transparency is important for selling goods without alienating the audience.

Traditional Marketing

While affiliate marketing is popular these days, there is still space for "traditional" marketing and ads to complement your podcasting revenue. Investigate the numerous podcast ad networks available — these networks will link you to advertisers and handle the information for you, but you'll need a sizable audience to get their company.

Suppose you have a smallish but loyal audience (under 5K monthly listeners). In that case, you can try to communicate directly with companies who want to reach your specific audience — particularly if yours is a niche podcast with an audience that might be drawn to items of a particular bent.

Charge guests to appear on your show

This isn't a monetization strategy that will work with many podcasts. If your appeal as a host is based on personal honesty, this can work against you. It can, however, be appropriate for certain forms of business podcasts.

If this fits what you do, consider selecting guests for your podcast for whom you can charge a fee in exchange for the exposure. It will be difficult to avoid making the podcast episode sound like one long advertisement, and you'll want to be open about what you're doing. Some podcasts, however, make this work.

Final Tips

Remember, without an audience, there are no sales.

Initially, try to concentrate on creating the audience rather than monetization. Since this move cannot be rushed, it is difficult to predict how long it will take the average podcaster to earn real money. Just keep in mind that once you've developed an audience, you'll have a multitude of options for making money doing what you enjoy.

In the early stages, focus on producing material that will appeal to listeners. Only after you have created a large amount of interest can you look into the monetization strategies discussed here. Before you can fly, you must first learn to walk!

Find your own way

Since no two podcasts are the same, no monetization formula will work equally well for all podcasters. This means that once you've created an audience, you'll have to experiment with various monetization approaches before you find the right combination of techniques.

Other Ideas for Your Online Side Hustle

Blogging

Blogging is an excellent side hustle work that can be done from home or anywhere in the world. It enables you to develop your personal brand while still owning your asset. You may also write about your interests. Starting a blog in a niche that you understand helps you reach out to an audience that shares your interests. Some popular niches for running a part-time blog include yoga, company, fashion, and cars. You can earn money by blogging in various ways, including affiliating links in your posts or linking to your online store where you sell dropshipping items.

How much money would you make doing this as a side hustle? You can make nothing at first. However, some bloggers who persevere past the first few years have made enough money to leave their day job to pursue blogging full-time.

Blogging Tip: If you love blogging, set up an online store that you can monetize and integrate a blog into it. This enables you to begin monetizing your asset before you have developed an audience. Furthermore, the combination of content and commerce is extremely efficient. As your blog increases in popularity, you can use retargeting advertising to monetize your traffic and generate even more sales. If you consistently produce high-quality content, you can have a few home-run posts that pull in a lot of traffic and are easier to monetize than if you were aiming for a few direct sales.

Information Products

If you're searching for a good side hustle to make extra money, selling information products might be an excellent choice. To thrive, this side hustle necessitates some analysis, time investment, and marketing skills. Are there any current hot topics about which you are well-versed? Did you come across a common subject on which there isn't enough information? Create content about these opportunities and monetize them. To begin earning money, you can publish books on Amazon or sell courses.

How much money do you expect to make from selling knowledge products? It is determined by the niche, marketing execution, and some other variables. However, a side hustle like this will bring in a few thousand dollars per month. The key is to produce a variety of content (ebooks, classes, etc.) that will continue to generate recurring income for you.

Selling Tip: With this side hustle, concentrate on niches where people have a significant issue that needs to be solved. If you're in the fitness industry, you could build a fitness workout course or a diet plan with recipes ebook. If people are urgently trying to address a pressing issue, there is an opportunity to add value by assisting them. The content you build will point them in the right direction. The best thing is that you will earn money when supporting others.

Instagram Influencer

When we're kids, we all dream of being famous. But the fact is that not everyone has the ability to sing or act. Fortunately, you can always build a personal brand based on what you can do. Maybe you have a great sense of fashion or can bake an amazing cake. Anyone can start a side hustle on Instagram by becoming an influencer. It's fine if you don't like being in the spotlight. You can develop an Instagram following based on your dog or your photography. You can monetize your Instagram account in many ways, including supporting posts, Instagram takeovers, and selling a product on your website.

Is it a healthy side hustle to be an influencer? The average influencer would charge between $200 and $400 per tweet. This can vary depending on the size of your audience, so feel free to look into influencer prices.

Instagram Tip: Be consistent with the type of content you share, the frequency with which you post, and the timing with which you post. People will follow you if they know what to expect from your page regularly. You won't be able to monetize right away, so focus your efforts on your followers by posting multiple times a day, every day.

Online Surveys

This isn't the most profitable side hustle, but it's worth noting because it's one of the simplest ways to supplement your income.

Taking online surveys means you're offering useful market analysis to businesses, and there are a plethora of credible (read: legitimate) survey sites available. Survey Junkie is one of my top picks. Signing up for the platform is easy, and you can earn money by completing short surveys about the items you use and your shopping habits.

Survey Junkie matches you with surveys based on the demographic details you provide after registering with the platform. You are compensated in points, which can be converted to cash through PayPal, bank transfers, or online gift cards.

Despite what some sites say, taking online surveys only pays $1-$3/hour. However, see it as a way to supplement your income when you're lounging on the couch watching Netflix or waiting at the doctor's office.

It's low-stress, mindless work. Just don't go in thinking you're going to make a lot of money.

Transcriptionist

Working as a transcriptionist is a side hustle that you can find on several blogs that concentrate on work-from-home careers. Transcription is the process of converting audio files into text documents. They pay close attention and write down exactly what they say.

They can work on general transcription jobs such as podcast transcription, interview transcription, web conference transcription, lecture transcription, or instructional video transcription. Transcriptionists who specialize in legal or medical transcription are in high demand.

Both transcriptionists would be required to type what they hear and then proofread it for accuracy. You can imagine how crucial consistency is to legal or medical transcriptionists.

People like this side hustle because it can be done remotely, has low start-up costs (other than decent headphones), and pays $15-$30 per hour.

Website Testing

If you're looking for a side hustle to supplement your income per month, consider website testing. In this activity, individuals with no direct connection to a brand spend time using, viewing and reviewing the brand's website to provide input on the site's functionality and appeal.

Website testing is invaluable in today's market, where websites play an essential role in the ability of both small and large brands to reach, engage, and convert online consumers. It is not enough to simply have a website; it must be optimized in such a way that it fosters positive brand relationships and eventually drives profitable conversions.

How much money do you expect to make?

Website testing is not intended to be a full-time job and will not substitute the entire income for most people. It can, however, augment your income and provide you with some extra spending money for the weekend, your next holiday, or a large purchase without depleting any of your savings.

In general, most website testing firms will pay you $10 per test, with the possibility of earning more on occasion. A standard website testing session lasts 10 to 20 minutes.

Where Will I Find Website Testing Jobs?

When you sign up to be a tester, the testing company will send you an email or list opportunities on its online site, and you must "claim" the test to gain entry. Depending on the number of users vying for openings, getting tests with certain organizations will be more difficult than others, and you will need to move quickly.

Here's a list of the best website testing platforms:

- UserTesting

UserTesting is a well-known name in the website testing industry. You get $10 via PayPal for every 20-minute test you complete and more for interviews.

- Userlytics

Userlytics does not need an audition to participate in testing. As a tester, you are given tasks and directions to complete when reviewing the site or app and providing input aloud. After your test results are accepted, you will usually be paid $5 to $20 via PayPal, depending on the project.

- IntelliZoomPanel

Most "studies," as IntelliZoomPanel refers to them, which are surveys, last between 10 and 20 minutes. Studies that require talking while reviewing through audio or video recording normally pay $10.

- TryMyUI

TryMyUI costs $10 per 20-minute testing session and allows you to record yourself on video and audio, as well as react in writing to a brief wrap-up survey. Each week, you should expect a few opportunities.

- Enroll

Enroll differs from other testing companies' websites mentioned above in that the assessments can be completed in a matter of minutes (as opposed to 15 or 20 minutes).

The payoff is much smaller because the assessments are shorter and take less effort. Payments are rendered monthly by PayPal.

Tips for Success

Here are some hints and ideas to help you make the most of your experience:

- Take the audition seriously

Almost any company would ask you to go through an "audition" before being paid to test their clients' websites. You will be tempted to rush through these auditions, but you will have a much better chance of qualifying if you take them seriously.

- Sign up for multiple sites

While you will eventually choose a company that you like best, signing up for multiple testing sites will provide you with more chances to earn money during the week.

- Be prompt to act

Most businesses offer tester opportunities on a first-come, first-served basis, so accept an offer as soon as you see it.

- Don't overestimate your potential earnings

Unless you have a considerable amount of time to devote to this side hustle, your initial earnings should be limited to $20 or $30 per week.

Six

SELLING SIDE HUSTLE IDEAS

Selling Printables on Etsy

As we have seen, nowadays there are many ways to make money online. The possibilities are limitless, ranging from reselling goods to completing surveys to finding remote jobs. Making and selling printables is one way to make money that has grown in popularity, particularly among bloggers. If you enjoy design, being a printable seller might be a great business opportunity for you.

When I first started selling digital items, I had no intention of selling printables on Etsy. I thought Etsy was just for handmade pieces and custom t-shirts, not for printables.

I wish I'd known what I know now earlier. Etsy is one of the best places to sell printables and other digital items online.

I've made a lot of money in passive income after discovering this and putting all of my efforts into starting an Etsy shop to sell printables. Selling printables on Etsy is one of my favorite online passive income streams this year.

Therefore, I'll show you exactly how you can make money selling printables on Etsy as well! But, just in case you're unfamiliar with digital products and don't know what a printable is, let's start there.

What exactly are printables?

Printables are digital products that are produced to be printed. A printable is something like a planner sheet or a coloring page. They are produced digitally and stored as a pdf or picture file, which can then be printed at home or a print shop.

Printables are the perfect place to start if you're new to making digital goods. They are simple to set up and provide a great source of passive income. Unlike other digital items, such as spreadsheets, they do not need any special skills or expertise to create. There are models and graphics available for use!

Why should I sell my printables on Etsy?

Why use Etsy when there are other places where you can sell printables? There are a few reasons why I think selling printables on Etsy is a good idea.

- Customers

If you don't have a website, Etsy is a great place to sell digital goods. Since it is a marketplace, you would have a pre-existing audience to which you will sell your goods. This is especially important if you don't have a website or a social media following. What's more, it's completely free to sign up and begin selling your stuff.

- Passive income

In general, digital goods are a great source of passive income. This means you won't have to exchange your time for money. Your goods will literally sell themselves while you sleep.

Since it manages the transaction and distribution of your goods to the consumer, Etsy makes it simple for you to receive this passive income. So, once your product is submitted, you simply don't have to do anything. That is the ultimate method of generating passive income.

• Easy advertising

Have you ever tried creating a Facebook ad or a Pinterest ad? It's complicated, believe me. The job is done for you when it comes to ads on Etsy. All you have to do is set a budget, and they will distribute your product to the masses.

Why do I say it's important? When it comes to selling your printables on Etsy, you want to meet as many people as possible. Advertising will help with this.

Another advantage of Etsy ads is that it is inexpensive. I've spent hundreds of dollars on ads on Pinterest and Facebook, but it hasn't resulted in any sales. You can pay as little as $1 a day on Etsy and see exactly how your ad is doing in terms of sales.

How to Create a Printable to Sell

There are so many different ways to make printables! For example, you can create whole printable planners, workbooks, goal trackers, printable quotes, posters, artwork and challenge cards ... There are so many choices out there for you! If you already have a blog or a company, printables can be a great product to sell to complement your blog or business.

As I previously said, making printables to sell on Etsy is an easy process. You can not only build them yourself using sites/apps, but you can also buy pre-made items and resell them.

My favorite methods for creating digital products are:

Canva

Canva is the first choice I would suggest for printables because it is such a great resource! Canva helps you create very professional-looking designs by using various online tools, models, fonts, and photographs. It's also totally free to use; you can pay to upgrade to the Pro edition for premium tools, but you don't need it to create printables worth selling.

Office by Microsoft

Microsoft Office has a few applications, such as Word and Excel, that are ideal for creating easy printables. Both programs enable you to make grids and tables if you want your printable to have boxes (for example, a tracker) or use specific fonts to build your own quotes.

The disadvantage of MS Office is that the design choices are relatively small, so I wouldn't suggest using it if you're planning on making printables to sell, but more for practice or to get out concept ideas.

Adobe Applications

Adobe programs such as Photoshop and InDesign can also be used to build your printables. These programs have a higher learning curve than Canva and are more expensive, but if you have a design background and understand how to pair fonts and images together, you can make some fabulous printables that are completely exclusive to you.

Affinity Designer

Affinity Designer is rapidly gaining popularity among graphic designers. Professional designers, artists, and creatives use Affinity Designer to create illustrations, logos, branding, UI designs, typography, print projects, mock-ups, web graphics, pattern designs, and concept arts. They can use the app to create precise curves, use vibrant colors, and customize live shapes for their vector illustrations. Affinity Designer also allows them to produce imaginative texts for headlines and advertisement body copy frames.

Templates

There are websites where you can purchase or download pre-made designs for a low or no cost. Here are a few examples:

- Creative Market
- Design cuts
- The CraftBundles
- The Hungry Jpeg

Best Selling Printables

I previously said that the real question you should be asking is, "What types of printables make the most money on Etsy?"

The list is potentially endless, and the only limit is your imagination. You can make money selling digital goods on Etsy, but you must be special! According to Etsy, the site has 2.5 million vendors, and as with any other marketplace, I suggest doing your homework before deciding what you want to sell.

And by study, I don't mean simply copying ideas. That is the easy way out, and it may land you in hot water. What I mean is, look at what's selling and figure out what's missing. You can also do the opposite: look at what's trendy and put your twist on it. If it's already a hot commodity, you'll have an easier time gaining momentum.

A good rule of thumb is to look for keywords with low competition but high search volume.

Here is a collection of printables that sell well on Etsy and could earn you a lot of money.

Babies

- Birth plans
- Baby shower signs
- Baby shower games
- Baby shower favors
- Pregnancy diaries

Wedding

- Bridal shower activities
- Bachelorette group activities
- Wedding invitations
- Wedding planners
- Wedding favors
- Cards with wedding tips
- Table identifiers
- Wedding To-Do List

Artworks with Quotes

Art printables are another excellent choice for selling printables on Etsy. Simply put, this is artwork that is sold to a client who can print it at home or a print shop.

You are basically selling the art file to them as a jpg or pdf. You are not required to send the artwork to them. This product category includes a wide variety of products, but quotes and watercolor art appear to perform well.

Coloring pages

Coloring pages have made a significant comeback in recent years, especially among adults. You can sell these pages for $1 or more to others so they can print and enjoy them. Moms particularly appreciate these when searching for activities for their children.

Planners

People adore planners, particularly when the planner sheets can be printed and reused repeatedly. As a result, consider creating a daily planner sheet or a monthly calendar.

Setting prices on Etsy

So, how much do Etsy printables sell for? Most single or two-page printables range in price from $2 to $5. When several printables are bundled together, they sell for more than $10.

The easiest way to figure out what price is right for your product is to compare it to rivals and simply experiment with different price points.

You can hold sales on products on Etsy. Consider selling the printable at the higher end of the market and seeing how it works. If sales are sluggish, consider holding a sale to see if it improves your purchases.

How to market your printables

It's time to market your printable now that you've finished it and uploaded it to Etsy. Though Etsy will help you get organic traffic, you will need to market if you want to see sales. I like to use Etsy advertising to help advertise my stuff. Again, you can run ads for as little as $1 per day on Etsy, and Etsy will drive traffic to your product.

Pinterest is yet another excellent resource for free product promotion. You can build pins that guide people to your product's purchase page. Don't forget to promote your goods on social media, your website (if you have one), and your email list (you must have one!).

Boost your sales

Do you want to sell more on Etsy? There are several ways to increase the sales of your printable goods. I've assembled a list of them for your convenience. Here are some ideas for increasing printable product sales:

- Bundles

By creating an Etsy package, you can group various items and offer a small discount to customers who buy the bundle rather than an individual item.

- Increase sizes

For example, if you sell planners, increasing the number of pages to a full planner allows you to charge more for the product as a whole.

If you're selling a baby chart, you can charge more by making it a nine-page printable instead of a one-page printable. One month per page equals nine more pages of money.

- More options

Increase the value of your items by including videos or a step-by-step guide on how to modify the printable. Including more content in the digital download would increase its value and ensure customer loyalty.

- Coupons

Who doesn't like a good deal? When you add a coupon code to your shop, your customers can receive a small discount when buying a printable. A good deal will lead to more sales and purchases.

This also gives your shop a more defined appearance. The more purchases there are, the more likely it is that other buyers would make a purchase. People have faith in what others have bought.

- Testimonials and reviews

People often buy from stores that have positive feedback, which is related to the previous issue. Be sure to solicit feedback from your customers.

When customers see the positive feedback from satisfied customers, the probability of them buying a product from you increases. They know the product is fine, which makes the purchase less intimidating.

Tip: Add picture feedback with your listings to increase credibility!

- Guarantees

You will encounter some hiccups with your customers, as with any consumer-related sector. Some stores have a warranty, such as a refund if the printing is faulty or sending an extra file if they mistakenly delete it.

Making your customers feel safe and cared for is good for business and your shop's reputation.

My tips to succeed

You now have the inside track on selling printables on Etsy. Just wait, there's more! Here are some hints to help you excel and, hopefully, sell the most digital products on Etsy.

Copyright

Etsy has stringent copyright infringement policies that you should be aware of. Violations of these guidelines may result in the closure of your Etsy shop, which you do not want.

Avoid taking ideas from other stores, and be aware of the copyright restrictions when using the works of others.

EtsyRank and SEO

For the best results, choose the keywords with the least amount of competition. This ensures that your item is not hidden on page 15 of the search.

Advertise on Pinterest

Pinterest is an excellent way to increase traffic to your store. To be honest, if it's a success on Pinterest, it'll almost certainly sell on Etsy.

Here are some great courses that will teach you everything you need to know about Pinterest

Handbook for Etsy Sellers

This is just another sure-fire way to guarantee your success. The Etsy Seller Handbook teaches you the best ways to run a good Etsy store.

Community

Learn from those who have seen firsthand the incredible success that Etsy has to offer. The Etsy Community contains motivational seller tales, event info, and the most recent community news.

Etsy Success Newsletter

Do I really need to say something else? You'll get weekly tips on how to expand your shop from top Etsy sellers.

My take away

You've got it now. A detailed guide to selling printables on Etsy. I'm not sure about you, but this seems like a great way to raise a passive income for a variety of reasons:

- It does not take much time.
- It just takes a few minutes to set up a store.
- You make sales without having to raise a finger.
- It is practical.

- It is easily available worldwide.
- You can purchase/download ready-made models to sell.

The list goes on and on. Selling digital art on Etsy is your ticket to making the goal a reality if you're looking for a fast and convenient way to keep the cash flowing.

Flipping Furniture

What if you could earn an additional $200, $500, or even $1,000+ a week by working a few hours on weeknights and weekends? You'd most likely sign up right now. It's a foregone conclusion.

Flipping furniture is a perfect way to supplement your income in your spare time. Best of all, you just need a few simple skills to get started, and you can start for as little as $150. As a result, it is one of the best side hustles you can start right now.

You can turn any piece of furniture, from kitchen tables to dressers and armoires, into a work of art that someone might be looking for. The "up-cycled" look is incredibly common among millennials right now, so this is a fantastic opportunity for you to capitalize on.

In the following pages, we'll go over how to get started flipping furniture, what you can do to make more money, and the best tips to get you started!

How much can I make?

The amount of money you can earn by flipping furniture is determined by several factors. How much time you have, how professional you are, and where you live will affect how much money you can make.

When it comes to flipping furniture, time is the most valuable asset. The more time you spend looking for and selling furniture, the more money you can make. E.g., you could spend 2-3 hours looking for a good piece of furniture to flip and make over $500 on that piece. Or you could spend an hour looking for a piece that will only net you $50. As with any other company, the more time and effort you put in, the more money you can make.

Most furniture flippers earn between $50 and $500 per month, but the best have been estimated to earn more than $15,000 per month with this hobby turned company.

How to start

You should know a few things before you start flipping furniture if you want to be successful. You'll need to decide which pieces of furniture are good candidates, what materials you'll need, and where you'll get your furniture.

What to flip

The best pieces of furniture to flip are those that are older and have a lot of character and flaws. It could be a dresser, an old side table, or any number of other things. When it comes to flipping furniture, the possibilities are limitless.

Look for high-quality products that display signs of normal wear and tear over time. These items can be refurbished and resold for a lot more than you paid for them.

Depending on your skills, you might recommend buying pieces in worse condition, but look for simpler pieces to refinish for those just starting out.

Where to search

Thrift stores and garage sales are two of the best places to shop for furniture to flip, but several other options exist. When anyone needs to get rid of furniture, they will frequently let it go for free if you can haul it away for them. Here are some places to start your search:

- Yard or garage sales
- Thrift Shops
- Craigslist
- Marketplace on Facebook
- eBay

How much to pay

Before making a bid, you can assess the amount of wear on your potential furniture. Traditional negotiation theory holds that you should always make the first offer to establish a low reference price and then negotiate around it. We recommend investing less than $100 on most of your pieces unless you have an exceptionally rare item that will be in high demand until refurbished.

Starting kit

To get started with furniture flipping, you'll need a few things. You may expect to use at least a few of the materials mentioned below, depending on the piece you want to flip.

- Transportation

Depending on the size of the furniture you want to flip, you'll need a method of transporting it when you buy and sell it. Larger pieces may necessitate using a truck or SUV, while smaller pieces may fit into a smaller vehicle. You should schedule your transportation based on the parts you want to flip.

- Working Area

This might seem obvious, but you can't flip furniture if you don't have a clean workspace! It could be your garage, basement, or even a spare room in your house; in any case, you'll need a clean place to work.

- Painting, reupholstering, and restoration tools

If you want to refinish furniture that needs to be painted or restored, you'll need some tools, which you can find at your nearest hardware store. Some of these elements are optional, but they may be useful to you (especially when just getting started). Here's my suggested list:

- Paint or Stain
- Wood Glue
- Steel Wool
- Rags
- Paint Stripper
- Paint Brushes
- Painters Tape
- Sanding Materials
- Sewing Machine
- Staple Gun

How to Restore Old Wooden Furniture

Now that you have all of the necessary equipment, it is time to begin "doing."

If you've never done any woodworking before, learning from people who flip for profit every day is the quickest way to get started and potentially make money over the next month. Flipper University, created by Rob and Mel of Flea Market Flipper, is the best course to take on flipping.

1. When restoring wooden furniture, you must first remove any old paint or stain from the item. This paint stripper comes highly recommended by me. It will make your work ten times easier! Apply paint stripper to the furniture and allow it to melt into the wood.

2. The stripper must then be neutralized by adding the appropriate spirit or polish remover and rubbing it into the wood in the grain

direction. Note: The paint stripper you use can specify if you'll need spirit or polish remover.

3. After rubbing your neutralizer into your product, inspect it to ensure it is free of any paint or stains. If there is some remaining paint, reapply the paint stripper and repeat the previous measures. If it's clean, wipe it down and set it aside for 24 hours to dry.

4. The wood would then need to be smoothed with sandpaper. If you discover a lot of rough spots, use sandpaper to smooth them out.

5. After the furniture has been cleaned and smoothed, you can add your preferred stain. Wipe away any excess stain and allow it to dry.

6. After the stain has dried, add shine with a finishing oil or wax. After each application, allow it to dry before applying another coat. The more coats you apply, the more gleaming your piece will be. Allow it to dry for 24 hours after you are satisfied with its sheen.

7. The final step in restoring wooden furniture is to apply a final coat of wax to the piece to add shine.

Reupholstering furniture

When determining whether or not to flip furniture, another choice to consider is reupholstering it. This entails fixing or removing the fabric on your piece of furniture to give it a new look and feel. Reupholstering furniture can be time-consuming, but it can also provide you with a rare opportunity to make money due to lower competition.

Expert advice

You're likely to make mistakes when you first start flipping furniture. We've gathered some of the best advice to get you started!

- No compromise on quality

When it comes to furniture flipping, you can always aim for high-quality items. After all, refinishing an Ikea piece that is a few years old isn't going to make you any money. Look for parts made of natural wood, such as oak and cherry (hint: they'll be heavy!). These items are more treasured and can sell more easily when the time comes.

- No rush, just follow all the steps

You would most likely be tempted to miss steps that are time-consuming or seem "unnecessary." To prevent errors, make sure to complete all of these steps, no matter how insignificant they might seem. This will save you a significant amount of time in the long run.

- Choose a proper workspace

Having a clean work area will prevent you from repeating steps while refinishing your furniture due to debris or dust accumulation on your item. It's also a good idea to keep your furniture out of direct sunlight to avoid bleaching while it's being restored.

Setting prices for refurbished furniture

After you've successfully refurbished your item, you'll need to decide how much to charge for it. It's a good idea to start by writing down how much time and money you've put into the piece. This should include the initial purchase price, any products used, any transportation costs, and any time spent working on the item.

If you've calculated how much time and money you've put into the piece, you can often mark it up by 200 to 400 percent. For example, suppose you paid $50 for a piece, spent $50 on materials, and worked on it for 6 hours total. You might fairly ask for something between $200 and $500.

An excellent way to assess your selling price is to look at what other similar items have recently sold for. If you find that a piece similar to yours has sold for a higher price, you can increase your price. You can always adjust the price of your piece after you've posted it. If you're not having a lot of interest, you can always lower the price and change accordingly.

You'll need to find a place to sell your furniture once you've determined how much it's worth. There are several options available, but some may be more affordable and easier to use than others.

Where to sell

You'll need to find a place to sell your furniture once you've determined how much it's worth. There are several options available, but some may be more affordable and easier to use than others.

- Facebook

Facebook Marketplace, where you can buy and sell products, can also be a good place to sell your refinished furniture. You'll have instant access to billions of customers, and there are no fees for selling your pieces.

- Craiglist

Craigslist is an excellent place to advertise your things for sale. It will take less than 5 minutes to list your item for sale, and users can easily contact you using an anonymous email address to make deals or ask questions.

- Garage sales

You may be able to list your refurbished furniture for sale at a yard sale. The benefit of hosting a garage sale is that you can also list other things in your home for sale.

- Antique shops

If you've ever been to an antique shop, you've probably seen a lot of revitalized furniture. Typically, you can pay for booth space, which allows you to view as many objects as you want. Some antique shops will charge you a percentage of your profits as well.

- eBay

eBay has been around since the early 2000s and allows vendors to sell goods to millions of online shoppers. What is the disadvantage of eBay? Many of your customers would be from outside of your immediate area, making delivery and transportation difficult. You may, however, mark your items as "Local Pickup Only," in which case the buyer would be required to pick up the item themselves.

- Your website

If you want to take your furniture flipping company to the next level, consider building a website to sell your products. You can start a website for a few hundred dollars per year or less, but it allows customers to access your items at any time of day.

- Social media

Anyone with a social media account should consider selling their things as a daily post. If you have a large following or a large number of friends and family, they will contact you directly on the platform to make a deal on your furniture.

Tips to Make More Money

There are a few things you can do to make more money if you're new or early in your furniture flipping business.

- Never accept the first offer

When you receive a bid, you will be tempted to accept it if it generates a benefit for you. If the bid is too poor, it is best to counteroffer or reject it entirely. Before selling your goods and accepting a bid, you should be aware of the costs associated with flipping them.

- Improve Your Productivity or Ability

As with any talent, the more time you spend flipping furniture, the better you will get. This will make you a more effective furniture flipper, lowering the cost of your pieces. This requires time and experience, so be careful!

- Promote Your Products

You will increase the value of your products by promoting them. If you only list your item for sale in one place, you limit the number of people who can see it and, as a result, make a bid. To increase your visibility and deals, promote your products through multiple channels!

- Reduce costs

Lowering the costs is the perfect way to make more money flipping furniture. This can be accomplished in a variety of ways. Maybe it's by buying in bulk or lowering your transportation costs. In any case, cutting costs will help you become a more successful furniture flipper.

- Save on supplies.

Spending less on supplies goes hand in hand with saving money, but we believe it deserves its own part.

You can easily invest a significant portion of your future income on paint and supplies. To save money, consider buying your supplies online through websites like Amazon or eBay rather than at more costly (but convenient!) small art or home improvement stores.

- Charge for delivery

Charge for delivery to increase your furniture flipping gains. If a customer falls in love with one of your pieces, there's a fair chance they'll be willing to pay a little more to get it shipped. Charging to get your things shipped is a simple way to make extra money.

- Show your products in the best way

How you show your pieces has a strong correlation with how much you will sell them for.

E.g., if you take a low-quality photo of your piece and list it on Craigslist or Facebook Marketplace, there's a good chance you won't get as much as you will if you took high-quality images or staged them in a way that enhances its appearance. This does not imply that you must have the most expensive camera. Make every effort to ensure that the images are appealing to potential customers.

My take away

Flipping furniture can be a perfect weekend side hustle for those with a few spare hours. You may believe that you must be handy or a strong woodworker to be good at flipping furniture, but this is not the case. Anyone with the right resources and time can become a profitable flipper.

Dropshipping

Dropshipping's success has skyrocketed in recent years. Dropshippers manage customer orders by linking a supplier to a buyer directly, eliminating the need to handle inventory. Today, this approach is used by 22 percent to 33 percent of online retailers, including thousands of people who have learned how to earn money online without high overhead costs. Dropshipping can be risky, but thanks to platforms like Shopify and Fulfillment By Amazon (Amazon FBA), it's easier than ever to get started.

Learning how to start a dropshipping company, like every other form of venture, is difficult. Nonetheless, it is an excellent first step into the field of entrepreneurship. You can sell to customers even if you don't have any inventory. You may not have to pay for goods in advance. And, if you are serious about your new business, you will build a long-term source of income.

If you're thinking about starting a dropshipping company, consider the following business and financial measures in this full dropshipping tutorial. Some are needed from the beginning, while others are just a good hint, but dealing with them now will save you time and headaches later.

What is the dropshipping business model?

Dropshipping is a kind of order fulfillment that allows store owners to sell directly to customers without stocking any inventory. When a consumer orders a product from a dropshipping shop, it is sent directly to them by a third-party supplier. The consumer pays the retail price you decided, you pay the wholesale price of the suppliers, and the rest is profit. You would never be required to manage goods or invest in inventory.

To sell the best dropshipping goods, you simply need to open an account with a supplier. There are two popular methods for finding a supplier for your dropshipping store:

1. By using a supplier database such as Dropship Direct, Alibaba, or AliExpress.

2. Using a supplier directory built into the store's backend, such as Oberlo.

Oberlo is the most user-friendly dropshipping solution for Shopify shops. You can use AliExpress to source millions of items from the Oberlo marketplace and import them directly into your store with the click of a button.

When a customer purchases something in your shop, Oberlo automatically fulfills the order. All you have to do now is double-check the order information and press the Order button. The product is then shipped to the customer from the AliExpress dropshipping supplier, regardless of where they are in the world.

So what do you need to do in this business model? You have to build a website and your own brand and select and promote the items you want to sell. Your company is also in charge of shipping costs and setting rates that result in a healthy profit margin.

How to launch a successful dropshipping business

Start off on the right foot

Dropshipping, like any other business, necessitates considerable commitment and a long-term outlook. If you expect a six-figure salary from some weeks of part-time employment, you will be sorely disappointed. You would be much less likely to leave if you approach your company with reasonable expectations about the investment needed and the profit potential.

When starting a dropshipping business, you must invest heavily in one of two currencies: time or money.

Investing time

I recommend bootstrapping and investing sweat equity in developing your business, particularly for first-time dropshipping entrepreneurs. I prefer this approach over spending huge sums of money for many reasons:

- You'll understand how the business works from the inside out, which will help handle others as the company expands and scales.
- You'll have a greater understanding of your clients and industry, helping you to make better decisions.
- You'll be less likely to waste money on vanity ventures that aren't vital to your success.
- You'll learn some new skills that will help you become a stronger entrepreneur.

Most people aren't willing to leave their jobs and devote six months to building their own online shop. It might be more difficult, but it is certainly possible to get started with dropshipping while still working a 9-to-5 job, assuming you set good customer service and delivery times for your customers. When your business begins to expand, you will move to work full-time on it as your cash flow and profitability allow.

Every business and every entrepreneur is unique, but it is possible to produce a $1,000–$2,000 monthly income stream in 12 months by working 10 to 15 hours per week on building your business.

If you have the opportunity to work on your business full-time, that is the best option for increasing your profit potential and chances of success with dropshipping. Concentrating all of your energies on marketing is particularly beneficial in the early stages when momentum is crucial. Based on our experience, a dropshipping business would typically require at least 12 months of full-time employment with a heavy focus on marketing to replace an average full-time income of $50,000.

That might seem to be a lot of work for a small reward, but keep these two things in mind:

1. If your dropshipping business is up and running, it will most likely require much less time than a 40-hour-per-week job. The dropshipping model's efficiency and scalability repay a large portion of your investment. The dropshipping model's efficiency and scalability repay a large portion of your investment.

2. When you start a business, you're creating more than just an income stream; you're also creating an asset you can sell later. When calculating your actual return, make sure to consider both the equity value and the cash flow produced.

Investing money

It is possible to start and expand a dropshipping business without spending a lot of money, but we recommend against it. We've tried both approaches to growing a company (bootstrapping it ourselves versus outsourcing the process) and have found the most success when we've done most of the work ourselves.

It is vital to have someone who is genuinely involved in the business's success in the early stages while establishing it from the ground up. Suppose you don't understand how this business works through every level. In that case, you'll be at the mercy of pricey programmers, developers, and advertisers who will easily eat up any profits you generate.

Of course, I'm not saying that you don't have to do everything yourself, but we strongly advise you to be the primary driving force at the start of your project.

You will, however, need a small cash buffer in the $1,000 range to get your company up and running. This will be needed for minor operating expenses (such as web hosting and dropshipping suppliers) as well as any incorporation fees, which will be discussed further below.

Pick your dropshipping idea

The next step in learning how to start a dropshipping company is to conduct market research. As if you were opening a retail store and researching various sites, rivals, and patterns, you can explore a niche you're interested in and make decisions based on how lucrative it can be. But the fact is that coming up with product ideas to sell is difficult.

Shopify curates a list of trending items based on the platform's top-selling product categories to help inspire the next dropshipping business idea. By concentrating on more niche and trending items, you can help get shoppers' attention and gain momentum without competing with larger, more developed businesses.

Niche products frequently have a more passionate customer base, making marketing to particular groups easier by increasing product recognition. Fitness, fashion, beauty goods, electronics, phone accessories, and yoga-related things may be good places to start dropshipping with no money.

Some examples of niche dropshipping stores include:

- Camping gear for campers
- Pet lovers accessories
- Laptop bags for travelers
- Fitness facilities

You may also use the following tools to test your dropshipping business ideas:

Google Trends

Google Trends will help you decide whether a product is moving upward or downward, as well as the seasons in which it tends to trend. It is worth noting that Google Trends does not show search frequency. So, if you use it, make sure to cross-reference the data with a keyword tool like Keywords Everywhere to assess the product's popularity in a quest.

Keywords Everywhere

This keyword analysis tool highlights the search volume on a monthly basis for your product and how competitive it is. You can use this data to gauge your dropshipping business concept's success and encourage new product concepts in the future.

Oberlo order volume

In Oberlo, you can check for items based on order volume to assess the viability of your business concept.

While the growth of e-commerce is a great boost for those looking to start a dropshipping company, it also generates a lot of competition. That means you'll have to conduct competitor research while developing your dropshipping business strategy if you want to sell your goods successfully.

Check competitors

Now that you've decided what you're going to sell in your shop, you'll want to look at who your rivals are and how they operate. Your competitors can hold valuable success tips and can assist you in developing a more effective marketing strategy for your dropshipping business.

Limit your research to only four/five other dropshipping firms, including one or two major players like Amazon or Walmart, if your market has many rivals (which is a positive thing in dropshipping). It will assist you in staying focused and planning your next move.

Some approaches to competitor analysis include:

Google search

Search engines are an obvious place to start. Make a list of the top five rivals using Google. Begin with main search words, such as "camping gear," in a basic search. The top ten results will reveal who the top rivals are and how they promote their products. If you want to narrow your search to a specific country, you can use a third-party tool such as Ahrefs or SEMRush to find keyword data in that country.

SimilarWeb and Alexa

These types of online tools are excellent for locating (and monitoring) the competitors' online operations. They provide you with information about your rivals' websites, such as their social media accounts, top traffic sources, number of users, and who their competitors are.

Social media

Look for Facebook advertising in your niche and study the market's top brands. Examine how the business interacts with its clients, the nature of its feed, the amount of engagement it receives—you can also follow its feed to never miss a beat. Use this information to help the company stand out and develop your social media marketing plan.

Competitors' mailing lists

Do you want to receive alerts from your rivals directly in your inbox? Sign up for their mailing list to get an inside look at their marketing campaign.

You will also find out more about the discounts and offers they use to entice consumers to purchase.

Learn everything you can about your main competitors' websites, costs, marketing strategies, product descriptions, credibility, and so on. Keep your study structured in a spreadsheet so that you can quickly refer to it when making store decisions. For example, you can keep track of your competitors' strategies in a spreadsheet, so you have it all at your fingertips.

Choose your supplier

Choosing your supplier is a crucial step in starting a successful dropshipping business. No sales business can survive without products to deliver to its customers.

You've vetted the goods you want to sell and know they'll be profitable—now you need to find a dropshipping supplier who can provide you with the high-quality service you require to develop. By connecting Oberlo to your online store, e-commerce platforms like Shopify provide a plug-and-play style alternative for finding potential suppliers.

Oberlo is an online marketplace that makes it simple to find goods to sell. Whether it's electronics, fashion, toys, or other hot things, you can find high-profit goods from dropshipping suppliers all over the world and add them to your store with a single click. The app handles order forwarding to your dropshipping provider, so you never have to think about packing, delivery, or inventory management. To begin, there is no cost.

The Oberlo app makes use of AliExpress to assist you in finding and adding items to your shelf. If you want to learn more about product quality, delivery times, or vetting a supplier, visit the Oberlo product page.

One thing to bear in mind: If your supplier is from China, try to sell Oberlo goods that provide ePacket delivery. EPacket is a low-cost shipping method for dropshipping goods from China to countries like the United

States, Canada, and the United Kingdom. Instead of waiting months for a shipment to come from China, the customers will just have to wait two weeks or less for a few bucks.

Create your e-commerce store

The next thing you'll need to get started with dropshipping is an e-commerce application like Shopify. This is where you can submit traffic, sell goods, and accept payments.

Based on my experience, I recommend Shopify because it's a full-service marketplace platform that lets you sell in multiple locations, including online, in multiple currencies, and manage goods and accept payments with ease.

You also don't have to be a designer or developer to use Shopify. They provide tools to help with everything from domain name suggestions to logo design. To change the look of your store quickly, you can use the store builder and Shopify themes.

How to market your dropshipping store

Now that you've learned how to start a dropshipping business, let's talk about marketing your new shop. When developing your business plan, you may want to put extra effort into marketing and advertisement to stand out in your market.

Since so many aspects of dropshipping are automated, you can dedicate more time to marketing and supporting your company in the following ways:

- Paid advertisements (Facebook and Google)
Facebook ads have some great advantages: they are flexible, brands can perform well on them, and they capitalize on people's desire to buy on the spur of the moment. You can use Google Shopping Ads to target long-tail

keywords where shoppers are more likely to buy. Google ads typically have more price competition, but it might be worth your time to try it out.

- Influencers

Influencer marketing is a form of marketing that relies on other people. As a new dropshipper, you may have a small marketing budget. Since people trust influencers more than conventional ads, influencer marketing is a cost-effective way to reach your target audience. Negotiate an affiliation fee with the influencer rather than a flat rate if you go this path. It's a win-win situation because they'll profit from each sale, and you'll pay less.

- Content marketing

Add content marketing to your dropshipping business strategy if you want to create a long-term traffic source for your store. Build content that entertains and educates your target audience by starting a blog centered on your dropshipping niche. You may also create a YouTube channel, infographics, or a podcast to help spread the word about your brand.

- Communities

Participate in groups of people who are enthusiastic about your niche. Conversations with potential customers can be started on Reddit, Facebook Groups, or online forums. When interacting with a crowd, remember not to be too pushy. Aim to assist and develop relationships with potential customers so that they can trust the brand and purchase from it.

- Mobile marketing

This is a general concept that refers to a business's use of mobile phones to communicate with consumers. Start a VIP text club, for example, and invite website users to sign up for exclusive offers and promotions. Alternatively, provide customer service in a live chat conversation with shoppers via Messenger. You can drive sales and revenue for your dropshipping company by creating automated lead generation, customer retention, and cart abandonment campaigns with a mobile marketing platform like ManyChat.

Keep an eye on which channels are working and which aren't, as with any effective online company, particularly if you're investing money in them, such as paid advertising. When the company grows and improves, you can still tweak your marketing plan to cut costs while increasing sales.

Keep improving your offer

After gaining sales experience and understanding the dynamics of dropshipping, you'll start to see the fruits of your efforts. Shopify analytics will assist you in answering some critical questions about your online shop, such as:

Sales

What are my top-performing sales channels? Where can I spend more money on advertising? What are my best-selling items? Who are my most loyal customers?

Consumer behavior

Do people buy more on their computers or their phones? What is each device's conversion rate?

Profit margins

Which goods and variant SKUs have the highest profit margins? What are my month-to-month sales and gross profits looking like?

Tools like Google Analytics and Search Console can also monitor search traffic over time and boost search engine optimization (SEO) efforts. Furthermore, suppose you use a third-party app for social media or

Messenger marketing. In that case, you can review the reports on a monthly basis to ensure that your overall plan is working for your business.

When building a dropshipping e-commerce shop, you can have a data-driven analytics system. Maintain consistency in your analysis over time, and calculate your store's results against specific KPIs. This will allow you to make better decisions for your store and eventually take your small business to the next level.

Other Product-Related Side Hustle Ideas

Flip items for profit

What is the best way to make money flipping items? Buy low, sell high, and then repeat. The formula is straightforward, but that doesn't imply that it is easy!

Start flipping without spending money

Surely you have many things gathering dust in your closet, attic or garage. Start with that. Free items can also be found on buy and sell websites such as Craigslist's Free section, Facebook Marketplace, and Freecycle.

You can even find free things to flip by digging through curbside trash, junkyards, and even dumpster diving if you don't mind getting a little dirty. You may also inquire with friends and family to see if they have any longer needed items. You'd be shocked how many people would give away their "junk" for free just to get rid of it.

Aside from that, junk removal is a legitimate side hustle as well. Perhaps you might also be compensated for locating inventory!

Your only weakness when it comes to discovering free things is your imagination. After you've exhausted all options for obtaining free goods to sell, you can look for bargains in other locations, such as auctions, flea markets, garage sales, and thrift stores.

What to flip for profit

Reselling is a common side hustle because it can be done by anyone and does not require a large investment. However, unless you focus on in-demand products, not every item you purchase would be easy to resell. Focusing your flipping efforts on more successful products allows you to sell more quickly and easily.

Your location and personal preferences, as well as transportation, shipping, and storage, will all have an impact on what you want to flip. It also helps to understand the worth of what you're selling, which is why it's best to stick to product types that you're familiar with and find interesting.

Here's a rundown of the best things to flip to get you started.

1. Clearance items

Going to the sale section of websites or local department stores to find heavily discounted products is ideal for buying low and selling big. The trick is to find highly desired and valuable products to make a profit after expenses.

Keep an eye out for well-known labels, seasonal products, and limited editions. Branded products are particularly attractive because consumers would pay more for brands they are already familiar with and enjoy.

1. Musical instruments

Musical instruments in proper working order are another thing to consider selling. Children and adults alike often outgrow or neglect their hobbies.

Once they've gone on, you can find cheap musical instruments to resell for a good profit. One Side Hustle Nation reader, in reality, created an entire eBay company by flipping guitars.

1. Sport memorabilia

Sports fans will still exist! Look for cards, autographed sports pieces, championship rings, ticket stubs, bobbleheads, retro hats and shirts, and jerseys.

These products sell well on eBay since people buy them as gifts or add to their collections.

1. Power tools

When it comes to flipping power tools, there is both demand and supply. Secondhand power tools are appealing to people who want to save money because new power tools are costly.

Look for items with recognizable brand names, as consumers often search by brand name. People sell their power tools when they are finished with a job, traveling, or purchasing a newer model and want to get rid of them quickly.

1. Kid gear

Without a doubt, baby items are costly. Furthermore, when children grow fast, they outgrow their clothing as well. As a result, frugal parents are frequently on the lookout for gently used baby and child gear, such as strollers, high chairs, clothing, toys, and so on.

If you have access to upscale children's clothing, specialty websites such as Kidizen cater to parents looking for designer products for their children.

Look for grandparents who are selling their young grandchildren's belongings. These items were most likely used infrequently at Grandma's house and are therefore in excellent condition.

1. Rare edition sneakers

If you're into shoe trends and fashion coverage, flipping sneakers might be right up your alley. Selling sneakers in the aftermarket entails purchasing the shoes at retail and immediately reselling them at a higher price.

This works because manufacturers do not produce enough sneakers to meet demand, resulting in a supply shortage. When it comes to luxury brands like Air Jordans, the resale market is fueled by high demand and limited supply.

Even though you will need some money to get started, sneaker flipping can be profitable and one of the best things to flip. Reselling sneakers help you capitalize on the popularity of a brand or a trend to gain access to an already established fan base and industry. No need to create your brand or following.

1. Top brand shoes
You don't have to be a sneakerhead to make money by reselling sneakers. In reality, there is a sizable demand for gently used name-brand shoes that are not limited-edition.

I know I've shopped eBay for specific models I wanted that had changed or gone out of stock.

Shoes also have the benefits of being small and light to ship, easy to clean, and readily available at deep discounts at yard sales and thrift shops. A pair can be purchased for as little as $5-15 but can sell for as much as $50-300, depending on the brand and condition.

1. Cars
Used cars are still common, whether as a hobby, a fixer-upper project, or a mode of transportation.

The aim is still to buy low and sell high, but in this case, you'll need a larger investment than in most of the other things on this list. Flipping cars works well as a side hustle for those who like the excitement of bargaining, finding undervalued vehicles, and are mechanically inclined.

Important! Several states have restrictions on car ownership and sales before you can legally register as a "dealer."

1. Technology

Smartphones, tablets, smartwatches, and computers/laptops are all highly desirable pieces of technology.

Not all hi-tech gadgets are made equal when it comes to the best pieces for flipping. Some brands and models, such as Apple's iPhones, MacBooks, iPads, and Samsung Galaxy phones, are much more common and maintain their value. You should expect to pay hundreds of dollars for these types of used electronics, with MacBooks costing thousands of dollars.

That is not to say that other brands and older electronics will not sell. People may wish to save money or obtain spare parts for old gadgets such as Nintendo game consoles. Any online research will give you an idea of what's common and what's not.

Craigslist, eBay, and Swappa are popular websites for flipping electronics, and the latter will help you determine the market value of your goods.

1. Vintage collections

Not all in the category of "vintage" is valuable. Value is affected by nostalgia, rarity, and demand. There are some brands and products that attract a lot of curiosity and popularity. Generally, the older the piece, the better, if it means it is rare, small, and often inaccessible in the public domain.

However, the value increases when you can incorporate objects like this into a package or a series. (Have you seen Storage Wars?) Pins, patches, sewing patterns, cards, coins, vinyl records, video games, silverware, china, watches, artwork, and dolls are only a few examples of collectibles that people would pay a premium for in a package or series.

Fans of classic brands such as Disney, Star Wars, Vogue, Barbie, the Beatles, Kiss, Hot Wheels, and Tiffany's are eagerly awaiting their next purchase.

Where to (re)sell

Now that you've accumulated some objects, it's time to sell them. There are numerous options, but here are a few popular online marketplaces.

- eBay

With over 160 million users, this long-running marketplace is the most successful. This gives you a lot of exposure for your pieces, but it comes with the sale and sometimes listing fees. (Learn more about how to make money on eBay.)

- Facebook Marketplace

Excellent for selling products locally, with no fees and no built-in payment processing. I used Marketplace to sell my old car, and the buyer paid cash.

- OfferUp

It is a free online trading app that focuses on local transactions. There are a variety of service fees, but none for in-person transactions. The app uses Stripe to process payments for shipped products.

- Craigslist

A relic from the early days of the Internet, this online classified ads website fuels many local sales transactions. There is no integrated payment processing, but the majority of postings are free.

- Mercari

It is a free app that allows you to sell new or used products directly from your phone. There will be no in-person transactions; all goods will be delivered. A payment guarantee and shipping insurance cover sellers. Listings are open, but there is a 10% sale charge.

- Poshmark

It is a free app that allows you to sell fashion and home-related products from well-known luxury brands such as Coach, Michael Kors, and Louis Vuitton. Consider it an online consignment shop. Selling rates are $2.95 for sales of less than $15 and 20% commission for sales of $15 or more.

- LetGo

A free online platform (app + website) for listing and selling secondhand goods in your region. Provides a chat feature for communicating with customers. Processing of payments is not included.

- VarageSale

This "virtual garage sale" platform is made up of groups where participants can buy and sell products locally for free.

Depending on what you need to sell, there are other interesting online and in-person marketplaces, such as forums, swap meets, Etsy, Autotrader (for vehicles), thrift stores, etc.

Seven

RENTING SIDE HUSTLE IDEAS

L ooking for a way to supplement your income without working long hours? Using what you already have to make money can be a great place to start.

Anyway, renting out your belongings isn't just an easy way to make money. It can also become a daily side hustle that converts your possessions into revenue-generating properties. Best of all, it can be a part-time job that doesn't need much of your time.

Benefits of renting

Before we get into the available choices, let's take a moment to discuss why renting your belongings makes a lot of sense. You do initially believe that you do not want anyone to use your land. That is one element to consider, but the reasons mentioned below might be enough to persuade you to give it a try.

- (Almost) Passive income

When you rent out your property, you can make money using assets you already own (passive income) rather than working more hours. You may need to invest some time in your side hustle, but it's not like you're exchanging time for money. If you have a busy schedule and no free time for extra work, this might be a perfect fit.

- Earn money outside of your job.

This could be a good match for you if you have a job and need something extra or don't have a job and want to make money from home.

- Make money from unused things.

You can transform anything that isn't being used into an income-generating asset by renting it out.

- Reduce the price of your products.

When you make money renting out an item, you can effectively cover the cost of purchasing it.

- Endless possibilities.

As you can see in this chapter, there are many options and several different items you can rent.

- Help people

Although it may not be the main reason for renting your products, you will be assisting others in saving money because they will not have to purchase the item for themselves. That's a plus, particularly during a difficult period when many people are struggling.

Airbnb

So far, we've seen many side hustle ideas, but they all need you to exchange your time for money. It can be exhausting, particularly if you already have a full-time job and are working late at night (or worse, waking up at 5:00 a.m. for your side hustle). What if you could make Airbnb hosting your next side hustle?

If you have a room you are not using or travel often and would like to rent out your entire home at some point, here are some hints to help you get started and determine whether Airbnb would be a lucrative side hustle for you.

Think about the space you want to list

The idea of sharing your home may sound appealing in terms of earning extra money, but you should think about what works best for you in terms of comfort.

Some Airbnb hosts choose to list their spare space, while others would renovate their basement. That is also a choice if you have a guest house. I've also seen some people rent out their unused boathouses, tiny homes, or RVs. Only make sure you have the legal right to list your room on Airbnb. Generally, if you own the land, it should not be a concern, but you should double-check.

You should have some simple accommodations for your bedroom, such as a bed and pillows, a place to store your clothes and towels, a first aid kit, and any other amenities you may think of.

When it comes to furniture, make sure it's all safe! Look around for the best furniture prices. Dishes, pillows, and kitchen utensils can be found at Target, TJ Maxx, and other outlet stores. Amazon Prime has excellent, low-cost choices for mattresses and televisions.

If you want to fix up your room before renting it out on Airbnb, you may need to invest some money upfront.

Set up your listing

To begin your side hustle as an Airbnb host, you must first build a profile and listing on the website and have it checked. Simply go to Airbnb.com and click on the 'Become a Host' button at the right. Following that, you'll choose the type of space you want to list, such as a home, apartment, or unique space.

When you set up your listing, be as descriptive as possible by sharing how many beds are included, how many people will stay, and whether there are any common spaces included, such as the kitchen.

The following phase in the process allows you to take some simple and well-lit photos of your room to be shown on the listing page. You may also add a title and a description to your listing.

You can be imaginative or direct in your word. Make sure to include specifics about the room, what's included, extra amenities, and the surrounding area in your description.

Setting a price and your availability for guests is the final step in creating your listing. Airbnb does an excellent job of predicting how much you will receive per month in your region based on the type of property you're listing.

However, since you can set your nightly prices, you have complete control over how much you receive. You may also choose whether you want to approve guests before their booking is verified or whether you want them to book automatically.

If you're just starting out, I'd suggest using the pre-approval process and simply checking in regularly to ensure that no one is waiting on you to validate their stay. If you are very busy or often travel, approving your guests first might also be the best choice.

Costs and fees

When anyone books a stay at your house, Airbnb charges a 3–5 percent fee, so keep this in mind when setting your rates.

You may also want to include a small cleaning charge to help you handle the costs of turning the room around after a guest departs to prepare for the next guest. Many AirBnB hosts can hire a cleaning service to clean the room after your stay or clean it yourself.

One advantage of hiring a cleaning service is building a good relationship with the cleaner and negotiating a monthly cleaning rate. If the idea of cleaning yourself sounds unappealing or you don't have the time, it might be easier to apply the cleaning fee and not think about it.

Overall, being an Airbnb host can raise your utility bills and household expenses because you may need to stock toiletries and replace other things as required.

Don't forget that paying a little extra to make visitors feel comfortable can be costly. I'll go into more detail about this in my next point, but you might need to buy furniture, new linen, coffee, and other items to improve the guest experience.

Positive reviews are extremely significant, and they can be the deciding factor in whether or not someone books a stay at your property.

How to make your guests feel at home

If you've ever stayed at an Airbnb, you've probably had either a positive or a poor experience. If you had a positive experience, consider why that was the case or what the host did to make it easier for you.

Airbnb hosting is all about hospitality and making someone's stay comfortable and enjoyable. Yes, you can make a lot of money renting out your room, but it won't last if you don't go out of your way to make visitors feel welcome.

Many people choose to fly with their pets, so you must decide whether or not to make your AirBnB pet-friendly. We've always been able to pay an extra pet charge when renting an AirBnB when we've taken our dogs on holiday.

Make a welcome guide

Some Airbnb hosts produce welcome guides for their guests when they arrive, which I have enjoyed when my hosts have done so. The guide is usually just a pleasant sheet of paper (possibly laminated) that welcomes the visitor to the home and shares a few important facts and information with them. Remember that your visitors might not know their way around, so it's a good idea to point out where things are.

The welcome guide you provide is a good place to leave your WiFi password and tell people how to contact you if they need to. You can also offer restaurant recommendations, transportation details, and local entertainment suggestions.

Place snacks on the table

You might also go the extra mile and have a small snack for visitors, such as bottled water, bags of popcorn, and chips. The small things make a big difference.

At the very least, you should invite visitors to make coffee in the kitchen in the morning and set out all of the required supplies. If you don't already have one, a simple coffee maker costs about $20.

Make yourself available

Some AirBnB guests leave negative feedback because they were unable to communicate with the host. Don't be a sloppy host. Traveling is often hectic and stressful, so responding quickly to messages and establishing an effective check-in process would benefit guests.

Even if you cannot be physically present during check-in, you can set up a lockbox or be very precise when instructing guests on where to obtain a key to enter their room. In reality, many guests prefer not to have the host present and prefer to communicate all information in advance via email.

Maintain an uncluttered environment

Even if you are renting out a room or the basement area of your primary residence, you can keep the space clean and clutter-free. Consider the concept of "less is more."

Don't overcrowd the space with furniture, personal things, or family pictures. Simply go with simple yet comfortable decor and keep it to a minimum while providing some basic necessities. You may also welcome visitors to any of your home's common areas, such as the dining room or kitchen.

I know that when I rent out an entire home on Airbnb, we like to feel at ease in the entire room. Remember that you can use your cleaning fee to hire a cleaning aid or reinvest some of your earnings in this job to save time on your end. It's well worth it.

There are so many people starting to side hustle as Airbnb hosts these days that it makes sense to give it a shot if you're willing to share your room. The majority of your work will be completed ahead of time when you plan your room and create your listing. You can simply update your calendar, set up an easy check-in process, and keep it clean and up to date from there.

Protect your mattress

This is probably my most important Airbnb host tip, simply because so few hosts do it. To avoid being too gross, consider the possibility of a hundred people sleeping in the same bed in your Airbnb over a year.

To keep the mattress clean for each guest, you can invest in a good mattress cover—one that fully encases the mattress. In reality, I get grossed out when I check into an Airbnb, and there are no mattress covers. Your clients may not inquire about it, but believe me when I say it's the first thing they think about!

Manage your AirBnb business efficiently

Plan your budget

We've already seen some of the costs involved in starting and running a renting business. When estimating cash flow as a real estate investor, make sure to account for these expenses and fees. In order to avoid unpleasant surprises when it comes time to do the math, it's best to plan a budget precisely. Although every Airbnb property is unique, in general, you can budget for the following expenses:

- Host fee

Most Airbnb hosts are charged a 3% host fee for payment processing.

- Maintenance fee

You must be prepared to pay for routine maintenance of the rental unit as well as the cost of fixing any harm caused by a visitor.

- Cleaning fee

If you use a cleaning service to help clean your Airbnb rental, those payments should be factored into your overall running costs. Turnover payments can include costs for basic necessities such as soap or toilet paper.

- License fee

Some local authorities require that you have a business license to operate your Airbnb business. These licenses are usually subject to periodic payment.

- Insurance

Airbnb provides its US hosts with up to $1 million in property loss insurance and $1 million in liability insurance coverage. However, it is necessary to remember that the liability policy comes second to the current homeowners and rental property insurance plans.

- Taxes

You will be responsible for paying taxes on any rental income earned from Airbnb, and you will receive a 1099 at the end of the year. However, you will be expected to pay state and local taxes, such as an occupancy fee, on the money you receive in some cases.

Manage guests expectations

Anyone who works in customer service knows that managing expectations is the secret to keeping customers satisfied.

It's fine if your Airbnb isn't perfect—just be honest about its flaws! Tell them if you don't want them to cook in your kitchen while they're staying in your apartment. Let them know if the upstairs toilet is prone to clogging and leave a plunger! If your Wi-Fi can be spotty because you live in the woods, be upfront about it.

Real estate agents are experts at transforming negatives into positives.

Become a Superhost

Notably, the Airbnb algorithm prioritizes hosts that have been designated as Superhosts. While the company does not have information about how much more Superhosts earn on average, it is reasonable to believe that they earn more rental income simply because they are seen more often when an Airbnb traveler books their stay.

With this in mind, here are some tips on how to become a Superhost:

- Increase your bookings
Airbnb Superhosts have a cancellation rate of less than 1% and book at least ten stays every calendar year or three reservations totaling at least 100 nights.

- Communicate often and promptly

Superhosts are required to maintain a 90% response rate, which means they must respond to 90% of all messages received within 24 hours. To make communication simpler, we recommend installing the Airbnb app, which allows you to communicate with a prospective guest even when you're on the go.

- Get glowing reviews

Because Airbnb considers guest reviews in their rating process, you should strive for as many five-star reviews as possible.

Make check-in easier

If you want to make check-in as simple as possible? You must purchase a keypad doorknob! This is convenient because you don't even have to be present when your guest checks in—you simply give them the code, and they can open the door to their Airbnb!

These are becoming increasingly common. They are now available in the majority of the Airbnbs I rent. Install a keypad doorknob instead of making your guests fumble with lockboxes or having to arrange to meet up with them at just the right time (which is a pain). For added protection, you can also change the code with each new visitor.

Maximize your income through upselling

Upselling is a term that almost everyone is familiar with. Congratulations if you've ever been asked if you want fries with your burger or seen those "people also purchased" recommendations while shopping on Amazon. You've been oversold.

Upselling is a powerful and reliable way to raise sales with little extra effort, and believe it or not, you can do it with your short-term rental. If you want to increase your earnings as a short-term rental host (and who wouldn't?!), here are a few suggestions for upselling your AirBnB guests.

Transportation

How will your Airbnb guests get to and from their rental? How are they going to get around once they've arrived? Purchase single-use public transit tickets in bulk and give guests the option of buying them from you before their arrival as one way to upsell your AirBnB. Alternatively, you can increase your income by renting out your car on a platform like Turo. Your visitors would enjoy the ease of not having to plan their arrivals and departures, and you will make more money as a result. That's a win-win situation!

Early check-in / Late check-out

Who doesn't want to sleep in a little later on their last day of vacation? What about those tired passengers who don't have to think about arriving at the unit on time? Offering the option of adding more time on the end of the stay can seem insignificant, but it is a bonus that many short-term rental guests appreciate. Those interested in this choice, according to Guesty, are willing to pay up to 40-50 percent of your nightly rate for convenience. What a fantastic and easy way to supplement your income!

Gift basket

A themed gift basket can be a fun touch for visitors who will celebrate a special event while staying at your short-term rental. You might, for example, sell anniversary or romance baskets containing items such as champagne, glasses, and chocolates, or you could put together something fun for those celebrating a birthday, holiday, or bachelorette party. A souvenir basket is another excellent idea for sparing visitors the time and trouble of going shopping. The options are limitless.

Local Artists' Work

Another inventive way to upsell to your Airbnb guests is to show local artwork in your home and sell it (at a profit, of course). Many visitors enjoy seeing things that they know were made locally and will leap at the chance to take something home to remember their visit. Are you an artist in your own right? Why not convert your short-term rental into a mini-gallery and sell some of your artwork?

Food/Alcohol/Specialty Products

If you've ever stayed at a spa or one of those boutique hotels, you've almost certainly sampled something from the minibar. Extra fees and add-ons, such as products bought from the minibar, generate an average of $2.25 billion in revenue for hotels. Why not extend this same idea to your Airbnb and reap some of the benefits? For example, my friend Micheal who runs an Airbnb in San Diego always tries to provide guests with the option of purchasing a bottle of wine from his personal collection, which they are charged for at the end of their stay. If you like this idea, you can also do this with food or other specialty products.

Most common Airbnb hosts mistakes

Host mistakes are a normal part of the Airbnb experience. Being an Airbnb host is a difficult job. You have a lot of responsibilities, and you must ensure customer satisfaction at any level. You will make mistakes while performing your duties as an Airbnb host. Some errors can be overlooked in the short term, and once they are corrected, you can move on. However, errors in the short-term rental industry have long-term consequences.

You're lucky that you're not the first Airbnb host. You can learn from the errors of others and study common blunders before making them yourself. Consider this: What if you learned ahead of time about all of your life's mistakes? Isn't it going to be easier to live peacefully? Similarly, this blog will assist you in effectively managing your house. Read, learn, and avoid making the same mistakes as others.

Airbnb host mistakes can become a stumbling block in your quest to become a super host. Airbnb has a predetermined requirement for choosing super hosts, and even a single error will knock you off the list of super hosts. As a result, it's best to plan ahead of time and try and make as few mistakes as possible.

Poor listing

The first step in starting your Airbnb company is to create a listing. You list your property and then sit back and wait for bookings. But have you professionally completed your listing? Guests can only book your property if your listing persuades them to do so. If your property description is unappealing, visitors may move on to another option.

The Airbnb property description should be creatively written and include all facilities, house rules, and pricing details. Anything on the listings, from photos to the calendar, should be up to date. You effectively communicate the facts about your property via the listing. Take your time finishing your listing and then waiting for bookings to get things going. If you've already mentioned the house, no worries; you can always change the details. You can use Hosty's management tools to view and edit all of your listings from a single site.

Unappealing photos

Airbnb images are included in your listings. Some hosts disregard the importance of photographs and post unappealing images. You are just thinking. Will you book a property that doesn't appeal to you? You must think like a visitor and then post images that highlight the benefits of your house. You can also hire a talented photographer to take beautiful pictures for you. It would be a worthwhile investment because images will affect future guests' decisions. A set of attractive images will provide the company with a competitive advantage. It is one of the most popular Airbnb host blunders.

Ignoring filters

Which do you prefer: a one-night Saturday reservation or a three-day weekend reservation? You can now tell Airbnb your preferences and set filters on who can book your house. Since 1-night stays will derail your long-term bookings, you can use the filter to set 3-day bookings as the minimum criterion. Similarly, you can use filters to prevent wasteful bookings. You must book only the best one if you want to increase your profit.

No Pricing Strategy

Your short-term rental should have a selling strategy, just like any other business with a financial plan. Listing your property on Airbnb necessitates an investment. Cleaning fees, cleaning fees, amenities, Airbnb fees, and so on. To make a profit, the pricing plan should cover anything while being fair for the guests. You must develop a pricing strategy that will allow you to grow and stand out from the crowd. Don't keep the same price over the year. As the seasons change, so does the demand for places, and therefore the pricing. Adjust the pricing based on the location's demand and competition. Do not take pricing strategy lightly; otherwise, you will find yourself at a loss after all of your hard work.

Not asking for reviews

Airbnb takes feedback very seriously, and failing to recognize its significance is a common Airbnb host error. It is just as bad not to get a review as it is to get a negative review. Positive reviews are your only choice for increasing your popularity and ranking on Airbnb search results. To get to that point, you'll need to ask your guests to rate your services. If you forget to remind them, you will also miss out on the opportunity to become a super host. There are various methods for prompting your guest to give positive feedback. You should review the visitor first, making him feel obligated to review you. You should contact them after you've checked out to say your final goodbyes and request a review. You may also submit a printed review form for a more customized experience.

Ignoring competitors

You are not the only Airbnb host in your neighborhood. There are over 7 million listings on Airbnb, with at least 3-4 in your region. You cannot afford to disregard your competitors and frame your plans without taking them into account. If you want to become a super host and expand your market, you must outperform your competitors. Investigate your competitors thoroughly. Learn about their pricing policy, services, and guest hist relationships. Adopt their strengths and exploit their weaknesses.

Not having a team

This is an error that the majority of the hosts see as advantageous. They believe that by doing it themselves, they can save money and therefore earn more. In fact, how can you produce quality results if you overburden yourself? If a visitor arrives at midnight, you would not be able to stay awake enough to send a welcome text. It would be challenging to keep the calendar up to date if you have listings on two sites. This could result in negative feedback and double bookings. There are some instances where a little assistance will result in better results. Consider it an investment. My favorite hosting management tool is HostApp. Its automation features will save you time and allow you to send triggered messages without disrupting your sleep. The integrated interface will effectively manage all of your listings and accounts from a single dashboard. The multi-calendar will keep your calendars up to date and avoid double bookings. Hosty app saves you time and energy to allocate it to more strategic activities of your side business.

Renting Your Car Out

If you work from home, seldom use your car, or want to downsize to a one-car family, renting your car for money might be a viable option.

After all, with the growing popularity of ride-sharing services and sharing your home via AirBnB, it should come as no surprise that people will want to rent your car as well, enabling you to earn some extra cash.

Why you should share your car

Who doesn't want to make some extra money? Even a few hundred dollars per month could help you pay bills, eat at great restaurants, and book more experiences while traveling. Peer-to-peer car-sharing, which allows you to rent out your car to others, is quickly becoming one of the best ways to supplement your income.

Here are a few of the advantages of car sharing:

- No investment needed

All you need is a less than ten-year-old car which has less than 125,000 miles and is in good working order.

- Minimal interruptions to your workday

Your "job" in car-sharing usually consists of keeping the interior of your car clean, removing personal belongings before making it available for rent, and driving it to and from the pickup/drop-off spot.

- Car sharing respects your schedule

You have your car if you need it. When you're not in your car, it's earning you money.

- Quick payments

Many peer-to-peer car-sharing systems pay you as soon as the driver returns your vehicle. Pricing and earnings are also straightforward, so you'll exactly know what you're getting for a day's rental.

- Vehicle security and customer service.

When you leave your car with major car-sharing companies such as Turo or Avail, it is clean, secure, and monitored 24 hours a day, seven days a week.

You will get insurance and access to customer service 24 hours a day, seven days a week.

Turo

Turo is the biggest peer-to-peer car rental marketplace in the United States. It gives car owners the option of earning extra money by renting out their vehicles to pre-screened and approved renters, as well as connecting renters with the right vehicle for their needs and timeframe. When anyone requests to use your vehicle, Turo provides $1 million in liability insurance and 24-hour roadside assistance.

How Does It Work?

It's simple to list your vehicle on Turo. You'll create an account, describe your vehicle, and upload some nice photos before creating a free listing. Turo can calculate a listing price based on your vehicle's market value, location, the current time of year, and other relevant information.

When anyone wants to use your vehicle, you'll be informed, and you can choose whether or not to confirm their request. The traveler can pick up your car at a predetermined location, or you can drop it off within a given distance.

Turo pays you via direct deposit within five days of the rental, and you can earn anywhere between 65 and 85 percent of the trip's cost. Turo has a mobile app where you can rate your rental car experience, and they currently have rental cars all over the world.

How much money can you make?

The Turo calculator, also known as the Carculator, can estimate how much you will earn per day for your car. You can search by location, but if your city isn't identified, you can get the average price for your car in the United States.

The Carculator begins by examining current market value from Edmunds or Canadian Black Book, as well as Turo's Automatic Pricing, which includes:

- Age and physical condition
- Style/trim, and features
- Convenience of pickup and drop-off
- Parking convenience
- Other Turo vehicles in the area

The Carculator provides just an estimate, and you can set your own pricing (minimum of $10/day) and turn off Automatic Pricing in the app.

According to Turo, Automatic Pricing would increase your earnings by changing the price to meet demand. Prices can vary depending on the time of year, day of the week, local events, and so on.

You can set weekly and monthly discounts to make your car more appealing to renters, and you can even accept custom price requests, particularly if you find a loyal renter.

You hold between 65 and 90 percent of your car's regular rental price. Turo retains the balance of the rental fee for insurance, roadside assistance, and customer service. According to Turo, US hosts earn an average of $545 per month.

If you sell Extras (which I'll discuss further down), you can receive up to 90% of the rental price. You are reimbursed in full for all expenses incurred by your landlords, including fuel replacement, fares, tolls, and cleaning or smoking fees.

Adding extras

If you're wondering how much money you can make with Turo, one way to maximize your earnings is to add extras. Adding extras boosts your earnings to 90% of the trip cost. For example, if I add only one of these options to my Subaru Outback, my take-home pay will increase from $36 to $43.

The following are some of the most common extras:

- Prepaid refueling or EV recharge.

Your guest is not required to refill or recharge your vehicle before returning it.

- No mileage limit.

Turo recommends pricing this as a per-day choice to account for wear and tear if your guests request and you accept a trip extension. If you apply the function to your listing, you will not be able to request it for reimbursement.

- Follow up cleaning

Your guest is not required to clean your car before returning it, but if you choose this choice, Turo will not reimburse you unless your car is extremely dirty.

- One-way trip

This choice allows guests to drop off your car somewhere else, but make sure you specify what is and isn't appropriate. You'll also need to plan ahead of time and budget for any costs associated with picking up your car.

Guests may choose whether or not to buy these extras, and Turo suggests keeping track of which ones they do so that you don't apply ineligible reimbursements.

The benefits of using Turo

Since I'm discussing this business as a side hustle opportunity, I'll concentrate on the benefits and drawbacks from the seller's perspective.

The biggest advantage I see in using Turo is the ability to gain extra money by putting your car to use when you are not using it. Earning between 65 and 85 percent of the overall rental price is a generous amount.

Turo has conducted research to determine how much you will theoretically gain by renting out your vehicle. For example, if your car is worth approximately $18,000 and you rent it out for 12 days a month, you will receive approximately $5,153 per year.

I also like how Turo assures your vehicle while it is being driven by someone else. Since you never know what could happen when you or anyone else is driving your vehicle, insurance is a must. The fact that Turo helps you to choose who can use your car appeals to me as well. They provide the vehicle owner with several choices and complete control of who can rent their vehicle. If you don't feel like renting your car one day, or if you believe the intended renter would go too far, you can always decline their order.

Bonus: For a limited time, Turo is offering a $100 bonus to vehicle owners who list and rent their car as a new host. Turo will measure 25% of your earnings for trips approved within the first $60 days, up to $100, to qualify for the bonus. To receive the full incentive, you must accept trips totaling $400, which isn't complicated given that even the most basic cars on Turo rent for $30-40 per day.

Drawbacks of using Turo

If you're looking for a stable side income, Turo might not be the best choice for you because you won't know who will want to rent your car and when requests may come in, making the income you receive unpredictable. However, if you are merely interested in establishing an extra stream of income that you do not need each month to get by, you might be able to ignore this.

Sharing your car can also come with certain risks. While the $1 million liability insurance policy is excellent, it does not cover substantial losses to anyone in extremely exceptional situations. The insurance package is tiered, meaning the basic policy has a deductible, while the regular and premium insurance policies do not. If your car is damaged during a rental and requires repairs, Turo will compensate you for lost rental income and also provide you with a temporary vehicle if you have the premium plan. These advantages are not included with the standard plan, so it seems prudent to obtain additional coverage for your car if you are concerned about the worst-case scenario.

My two cents

Turo is going to be easy money for the right people. It only takes 10 minutes to list your vehicle, and the Turo app makes it simple to manage your listing and communicate with visitors. The truth is that your car is a depreciating commodity, so why not try to make some extra money with it?

Other rental side hustle ideas

A rental company can be a very profitable side hustle that eventually grows into something you can do full-time. It also leverages assets you already own or needs a relatively small investment to purchase equipment. The majority of the ideas below need less than $200 to get started. And in several instances, after only a few leases, you've already repaid your initial investment. It's all benefit from there. This means you've got a pretty sweet setup, low-investment, high-profit business ideas.

RV

RVs are becoming increasingly common. People want to have memorable experiences cost-effectively. Owning and renting out an RV is an excellent way to supplement your income while capitalizing on this rapidly rising trend.

The cost varies. Many people who are new to the RV scene already own an RV that is frequently underutilized.

Potential rental income: $100+ a day

Car seat

If you have children, you know that installing a car seat is one of the most aggravating tasks in life. I've seen decent churchgoers swear aloud after failing to mount a car seat.

When traveling out of state with children, the issue of 'what are we going to do about car seats?' eventually arises. We recently had a few couples from out of state visit us, and they all brought their toddlers. We wanted three car seats and ended up renting them from a small business in the neighborhood. We saved about half the price of a new car seat and avoided all of the installation hassles. If we had purchased three car seats, the cost would have been much higher, we would have had to find out where to store the heavy buggers, and we would have had to deal with the installation.

Renting car seats addresses all of these problems while still providing a substantial benefit to the rental company owner.

Price: $100 or more

Rental potential: $35 or more a day

Snow equipment

If you can coordinate with your neighbors, this might be a good option. Instead of anyone purchasing their own snowblower, they can just use yours when it snows. You'll store it, maintain it, and refuel the blower. In exchange, they pay you money to use their services. If you have many neighbors, this can quickly add up. Their lives are made simpler, and you benefit as a result.

Price: $150 and up

Potential rental income: $100 per season

Bike

If you have an extra bike? Why not try renting it? Making a post on Nextdoor is an excellent way to spread the word. I wouldn't purchase a bike solely for rental purposes because you'd be competing with bike rental systems in more densely populated areas.

Price: $200 or more

Rental potential: $20 or more a day

Childproofing supplies

Childproofing is another growing trend. Families are rightly taking better precautions to prevent children from getting hurt due to the dangers present in each home. This rental idea could be useful for both the main house and a vacation spot. Even more than a stroller, you really don't want to carry a baby gate to your in-laws' beach house.

Cost: $75+ per item, depending on quantity

Rental potential: $15 a day or more

Music instruments

Many of my fellow guitarists have several instruments, many of which are seldom used. Renting them out (especially to new players) is a great way to make money from something you don't use very much.

Price: $350 and up

Rental income potential: $50 a week

Moving equipment

Many do-it-yourselfers out there do not want to pay a moving company to carry their belongings.

However, even though you are on a tight budget, having the right equipment would make the job of traveling much easier. It's worth saving a few dollars to find the right equipment, which is still much less than the cost of hiring a moving company. Given that most people travel infrequently, it is unlikely that they have or will choose to purchase any of this. As a result, renting out moving equipment is another excellent business concept. I'm referring to stuff like moving dollies, hand trucks, shoulder straps, etc. None of this equipment is particularly costly, and it comes in handy when it comes to traveling.

Price: $200 or more

Potential rental income: $100+ a day

Bounce house

Bounce houses are loved by kids, especially at birthday parties. Many parents don't want to have one permanently in their backyard but are instead willing to rent one when they have to hold some event for their kids. You can combine this with some other children's games and activities and cater to birthday parties in your neighborhood to create a profitable rental company.

A commercial-grade bounce house will cost you at least $600.

Rental potential: $150 or more a day

How to start your rental side hustle

I've given you lots of ideas, but you may be wondering how to get started. Here are six simple steps to start your own rental business:

- Identify your niche

Choose one of the niches I've listed or make up your own. The important thing is that it's related to something that's in demand.

- Get your stuff

Get the equipment you want to rent and make sure it is of good quality. Try to find out all the features of the equipment (how it works, how to set it up, how to use it, etc.) so that you can answer questions from potential customers.

- Set your price

I'd think about a few things when it comes to pricing. To begin, how much does it cost to buy new? Second, how difficult is it to set up and store the item? Third, what are comparable objects rented for? After taking these considerations into account, you should be able to find a reasonable price.

- Marketing the rental company

There are different approaches to this topic, and everyone has to find their own way. Personally, I highly recommend using Nextdoor.com. It is the perfect social network for establishing a local rental company. If you're not familiar with it, it's a social network made up of people in your neighborhood, many of whom are excellent prospects for your company.

Craigslist is another free way to get the word out. Also, you should network with people in your area who might be able to provide you with good contacts (e.g., handymen, party planners, photographers, etc.).

- Service

Your rented products can break or wear out over time. Be sure to service or replace them regularly to keep users safe and happy.

- Repeat it and make a profit

Once you have everything up and running, you can simply rinse, repeat and start profiting from your newfound side hustle. The fact that many of these ideas only require a handful of rentals to pay off makes the whole model very appealing. Believe me, you can make a lot of profit through rentals!

Eight

CONCLUSION

O ur lives have been turned upside down by the pandemic, and conventional jobs have changed drastically. Throughout the era of COVID, we have witnessed the rise of independent workers. It took a pandemic, but the side hustle has finally been accepted in the public attitude as a "serious" job.

Even before COVID, independent contractors were a rising part of the U.S. labor force; one pre-pandemic estimate put the gig economy at more than a third of all workers. Their incomes and participation will have increased by 33% by 2020.

This change in power dynamics is critical to the growth of self-employed workers. The pandemic inspired people to focus on new ideas regarding their workplace. Millions of people started doing online jobs, creating online content and much more from their homes, as the pandemic was there to stay for some time.

According to a new recruiting survey, 92 percent of respondents believe now is a good time to look into gig jobs. More than half of those polled said they would prefer a long-term contract with flexible hours. Even as Americans slowly return to in-person jobs, this need for flexibility persists.

Start Your Side Hustle aims to satisfy the curiosity of those who have decided to reset their lives, prioritizing certain personal values over their careers. We have seen how the list of opportunities is almost endless, and the only limits are our creativity and desire to work hard for our future.

Side hustles can be viewed as a means of having some extra money each month to pay the bills. But we've seen how some of them can become not only the main job but also a real business on which you can establish a company.

Now you have all the information you need to start building your financial freedom, make good use of it.

Good luck!

www.ingramcontent.com/pod-product-compliance
Lightning Source LLC
Chambersburg PA
CBHW071655210326
41597CB00017B/2220